MASTER THE ART OF
Winning

THIS BOOK BELONGS TO:

....

IF FOUND, PLEASE CONTACT:

....

Copyright © 2022, Donene Taylor
All rights reserved.

No part of this book may be used or reproduced in any manner whatsoever without written permission except in the case of brief quotations embodied in critical articles and reviews.

Requests for authorization should be addressed to:
Donene Taylor, PO Box 504, Glenrock, Wyoming 82637
or **DoneneTaylor@gmail.com**

Cover Illustration by **Roper Taylor**
Illustrations on pages 258, 276, 300, 320 by **Matej Beg**
Cover design by **Ivica Jandrijevic**
Interior layout and design by **Writing Nights. www.writingnights.org**
Book preparation by **Chad Robertson**

ISBN: 978-1-7330676-1-4

LIBRARY OF CONGRESS CATALOGING-IN-PUBLICATION DATA:
NAMES: Taylor, Donene, author
TITLE: Master the Art of Winning / Donene Taylor
DESCRIPTION: Wyoming: One Spotted Pony Publishing, 2022
IDENTIFIERS: ISBN 978-1-7330676-1-4 (Perfect bound) | 978-1-7330676-3-8 (Case Bound)
SUBJECTS: Confidence | Breakaway Roping | Mental Performance | | Rodeo | Coaching | World Champion
CLASSIFICATION: Pending
LC record pending

One Spotted Pony Publishing
Printed in the United States of America.
Printed on acid-free paper.

MASTER THE ART OF *Winning*

A CHAMPIONSHIP PLAYBOOK
TO OPTIMIZE MENTAL PERFORMANCE

DONENE TAYLOR
WPRA World Champion

To my husband, Stan.

*Thank You for helping me to embrace the mindset
that everything is training for something.*

*I appreciate you challenging me to
live consistently outside of my comfort zone.*

*Moment to moment to moment,
I love you with my whole heart.*

CONTENTS

Acknowledgements 11

Introduction 13

PERFORMANCE RESULTS RECORD 19

DAILY PERFORMANCE JOURNAL PAGES 25

MY NOTES 215

THINGS I CAN CONTROL vs THINGS I CANNOT CONTROL DRILL 227

RECOGNIZING SIGNAL LIGHTS DRILL 231

CONFIDENCE CONDITIONING STATEMENTS DRILL 237

IDENTIFYING MY GREATNESS A – Z DRILL 253

BUILDING A CONFIDENCE RESUME DRILL 257

BUILDING A SUCCESS CHECKLIST DRILL 275

BUILDING PERFORMANCE ROUTINES DRILL 287

**TECHNICAL PERFORMANCE AND
MENTAL PERFORMANCE BASIC SKILLS DRILL** 299

BUILDING A WHOOP PERFORMANCE GRID DRILL 313

EQUIPMENT AND ESSENTIAL SUPPLY INVENTORY 319

Get to Know the Author 328

THE MAN IN THE ARENA

"It is not the critic who counts; not the man who points out how the strong man stumbles, or where the doer of deeds could have done them better. The credit belongs to the man who is actually in the arena, whose face is marred by dust and sweat and blood; who strives valiantly; who errs, who comes short again and again, because there is no effort without error and shortcoming; but who does actually strive to do the deeds; who knows great enthusiasms, the great devotions; who spends himself in a worthy cause; who at the best knows in the end the triumph of high achievement, and who at the worst, if he fails, at least fails while daring greatly, so that his place shall never be with those cold and timid souls who neither know victory nor defeat."

—THEODORE ROOSEVELT

Acknowledgements

To my husband, **Stan**, I'm so grateful for your unconditional love, support, and encouragement, as I rundown what sets my soul on fire. Your belief in me and my Bold Goals warms my heart, especially when I see you believing in my goals, as if they were your own. Our life together is still that wild and fun adventure it was thirty years ago! Thank you for your continued encouragement to keep reinventing myself to do new and interesting things. You are the best thing in my life!

To my son, **Roper**, thank you for sharing your illustration talents with me, which brought this book cover to life. It means the world to me that you took time to understand my purpose and passion for writing it. You clearly captured the heart and spirit of this book with the cover. Daily, each of us sorts out the pieces of our own, unique life "puzzle." Even after diligent work, when the prize is attained, the "puzzle," continues because our life has no finish line, until the last breath. It takes extreme fortitude and courage to keep taking the next, best step forward toward Bold Goals. I love you to the moon and back a gazillion, million times.

To **Holly DeLaune**, owner of Firebrand Marketing, thank you for your kind and persistent encouragement to write my second book. I am extremely grateful that you interpreted my first few "no" responses as "not right NOW." I whole heartedly appreciate you speaking transformational possibilities into my life. You and your fabulous Firebrand Marketing team boldly make my entrepreneur visions come to life. Thanks for going "all in" with me on this book and making it super special, with all the extra sparkle and shine. Your friendship means the world to me, and my life is much more exciting with you in it!

To **Chad Robertson**, owner of Writing Nights, I appreciate the time, expertise, and attention to detail you and your wondrous Writing Nights team has shared with me once again. Having you in my elite, inner circle makes my life much richer, fuller—and fun! You continue to grow my mind, my heart, and my vocabulary. From my whole heart, I thank you for taking me as I am, being my friend, and helping me get another book across the "publish line." You exceeded my expectations with your extraordinary work!

To **Trevor Brazile**, 26-time PRCA World Champion, thank you for allowing me to come to your ranch for one-on-one coaching. My goal in working with you was to level up my horsemanship and roping performance with Chester. I remember asking you, "What is one thing I can do, to get better?" My life was forever transformed by your thoughtful answer. The gift, of you speaking into my life, had great influence in how I finished this book. It has inspired me to choose differently how I show up for myself. From my whole heart, I appreciate you!

To my **Amazing Clients**, those I have already coached, and those I will coach in the future, many thanks for growing me, making me dig deeper, and encouraging me to work towards my optimal best—just as I encourage you to do.

I love what Proverbs 27:17 says. "As iron sharpens iron, so one person sharpens another." Did you know that the piece of iron or alloy that is used to sharpen another piece of iron must be made with an edge that is of a harder and rougher texture? The harder, rougher alloy provides the resistance needed to sharpen the dull blade.

This is why it is incredibly important to include people in your elite, inner circle who will challenge you, test you, and coach you up. This sharpening process may be uncomfortable, challenging, and difficult. I have found that when you have an elite, inner circle who cares for you, cheers for you, and wants you to level up, this sharpening process comes from their heart.

It keeps me fired up to know that we are all sharpening each other, along the way – my clients, my competitors, and me. We are all working toward the common goal of success, defined as relentlessly pursuing the best version of ourselves. We are better today than we were yesterday. We will be better tomorrow than we are today. All the while, working toward worthy goals and ideals. I sincerely thank you for adding fuel to my fire and giving me opportunities to become the best, moment to moment to moment. The blessings of coaching Mental Performance and competing, in a sport I love, give me an enormous amount of joy.

Introduction

WELCOME!!

I am extremely excited for you and the journey you're ready to embark on, over the next few months. *Master the Art of Winning: A Championship Playbook to Optimize Mental Performance* is one-of-a-kind. Inside your *Performance Journal*, you will find my mental performance playbook of drills. These drills will help you work toward the person you are designed to become, while achieving your Bold Goals and *Mastering the Art of Winning*.

In my previous book, *Heart of a Champion*, I share my mental performance playbook of how I accomplished my Bold Goal of winning a World Championship in the WPRA at 52 years of age. I set this Bold Goal at age 14, and it evolved into a 38-year mission and a phenomenal journey of self-discovery.

I get asked frequently, "How did you achieve your Bold Goal to become a World Champion?" My answer is that, "It began with setting a daily goal of becoming the best at getting better."

Becoming the Best at Getting Better Requires:
- Gathering, documenting, measuring, and evaluating data
- Brainstorming, solution finding, and creativity
- Investing time to reflect and refocus
- Taking consistent action

Master the Art of Winning: A Championship Playbook to Optimize Mental Performance provides you the opportunity to meet each of the above requirements to become the best at getting better. I am extremely excited to share my *Performance Journal* with You! I believe you can be a Bold Goal setter and a Bold Goal getter.

HOW TO START

"It is the start that stops most people."
—**DR. ROB GILBERT**

Staying committed and being consistent by writing in your *Performance Journal* is easy to do, but it can be easy NOT to do.

3 Simple Strategies for Consistent Journaling Success:
1. Set your daily intention to journal. Include journaling into your daily habits and routines of excellence. Keep your journal and pen in a location where you will see it daily and have easy access to it. Seeing your journal is the "SPARK" for you to journal each day.

2. Schedule your intention to journal. What gets scheduled gets done. To be consistent, you must commit to a schedule. This is a "draw a line in the sand" moment. I want to encourage you to do just that. Draw a line in the sand, step across it, and tell yourself, "At this time of the day/night, I journal; no matter what."
3. Select your special place or places to journal. I have found a quiet place gives me the opportunity to relax, quiet my mind, and be open-minded. I like to journal sitting on my bench in my barn. I call this my "Thinking Chair."

I commit to journaling in the morning and evening. I invest a minimum of 15 minutes a day journaling. The time I invest journaling may vary, depending on my headspace and the journaling goal I have set for that day.

As you open up your brand new *Performance Journal*, you may have thoughts of:
- I don't want to make a mistake writing in it.
- What if I mess it up?
- I need to do it right the first time.
- I must keep it neat and orderly.
- I will wait until the first of the week, next month, beginning of my season, or the first of the year, before I begin using it.

Should this be your mindset, I want to encourage you to eliminate this unproductive thinking from your mind immediately.

I want to challenge you to shift your mindset to this instead. Mistakes, mess ups, doing it right, keeping it neat, or waiting till the perfect time does not exist, while keeping this *Performance Journal*. This *Performance Journal* encourages do-overs and provides multiple opportunities to learn, grow, and evolve.

Here's the deal, and this comes from my heart. The only way you can mess this up is by NOT DOING IT.

> *"Think left and think right and think low and think high. Oh, the thinks you can think, if only you will try."*
> **—DR. SEUSS**

WHY DO IT

> *"The definition of insanity is doing the same thing over and over and expecting different results."*
> **—ALBERT EINSTEIN**

There is a plethora of reasons I can give you, as to why you want to keep a performance journal. I am passionate and purposeful about keeping one because I have experienced firsthand the transformational benefits it provides.

The Following are My Reasons for Encouraging You to Journal:
- Putting pen to paper gives you a place to organize your thoughts and productively assess your performance. Writing in this journal gives you the opportunity to reframe your thoughts productively, and use your situation to your advantage, even when the journaling session may begin with thoughts that are unproductive.
- This is a **"Keep It Real Zone."** What this means is there is absolutely, positively,

NO BLAMING, COMPLAINING, JUDGING or COMPARING allowed here. I am challenging you to do things differently this time and to own everything, which gives you power to change it.
- Think of yourself as a scientist. Scientists keep it really real. They conduct experiments, collect the data, evaluate the results, reflect how they can do it better, refocus with clarity, perform the new experiment, and **WIN** the next moment. Lather, rinse, repeat. Your *Performance Journal* is like a scientific notebook and contains valuable information.

I really wanted to be a World Champion for decades. At the beginning of each season, I showed up with enthusiasm. I believed with my whole heart, "This will be the year I win it!" However, I was going about it all wrong. I approached each new season the same way as I did the previous season. I unrealistically believed the new season would magically be different than the season before. I did this season after season after season. I was on an insanity loop.

The pivotal moment for me, in understanding the importance of keeping a *Performance Journal,* was when I grasped the definition of insanity. I write about this transformational story in my book, *Heart of a Champion.* Embracing the cold, hard truth that I was on an insanity loop was the trigger point for me to implement and keep one.

Performance journaling shifts your perspective and lets you zoom out to see the big picture. Doing this allows you to see your available options. The journal will help you ask yourself thought-provoking and productive questions, which will help you find solutions, put a plan in place, and take action. A question that I ask myself frequently is: "What is the next, best step I can take that will help me move forward?"

In my journey of running down Bold Goals, I have had competence of the required skills, without being in a confidence state. The reverse has also been true. Each of these situations limited my potential to perform optimally.

Maintaining this *Performance Journal* and working each drill gives you multiple opportunities, over the few months, to build the bridge that connects your confidence and competence.

This journal provides you a place to **CELEBRATE YOU!** It gives you an opportunity to gain awareness of all your progress, strengths, wins, and accomplishments. Big and small, you are going to **CELEBRATE THEM ALL!**

Unpack each of your lessons and learns by identifying what you can do better and investing time building out how you can do it differently. This growth mindset will launch you to the next level.

> "Do the best you can, until you know better. Then, when you know better, do better."
> —MAYA ANGELOU

WHAT'S INSIDE

"What is deeply rooted inside of you, shows up in all you do."
—DONENE TAYLOR

Inside this *Championship Playbook* are transformational drills that will give you the opportunity to Reflect – Refocus – Perform – Win. The spirit in providing you multiple open journaling pages for each of these drills is to encourage you to revisit, revise, and rework these drills.

Over the next three months, as you rework these drills, you will learn more about yourself, your process, and your journey because you will be in a different place in life each time you do the drill.

The spirit of doing these drills is to encourage and challenge you to think outside of the box, do the extra work, and introduce yourself, to the you that you have never known before.

Here is what you will find inside your *Performance Journal.* As you embrace each drill and give them your full effort, the lessons you've learned will become deeply rooted inside of you.

1. **Three months of reflective journaling pages, with unique prompts,** are foundational in gaining awareness of and evaluating your performance. The prompts are designed to spark you. To help identify strategies you want to implement and the action you want to take.
2. **Extraordinary mental performance drills provide you with many opportunities to develop:**
   - Locked-In Focus
   - Productive Perspectives
   - Excellent Daily Habits and Routines
   - Exceptional Organizational Skills
3. **Proven strategies are presented to fill your confidence tank** despite the events you are experiencing, the results you are (or are not) getting, and no matter the drama, distractions, noise, or chaos that is going on around you (or inside of you).
4. **A framework is provided to rundown your Bold Goals.** There are numerous opportunities provided to strategically train, with your end goal in mind. Reverse engineering Bold Goals is crucial, to accomplish them. Bold Goals do not happen by accident. They happen with intention.

Completing this *Performance Journal* is a three-month process. At the end of these months, as you complete the final line on the last page, you will not be the same person, nor will you be in the same place as you were three months ago. You will have gained self-awareness, developed new strategies, and taken an enormous amount of action.

THINK BIG!

There are no rules in using your *Master the Art of Winning: A Championship Playbook to Optimize Mental Performance.* I designed it with the spirit of giving you ample space to **THINK BIG!** I encourage you to diagram, draw, use bullet points and arrows. Use colorful pens and pencils. If writing in complete sentences is how you **THINK BIG** the best, do lots of that! You are writing the stories of your journey. Your journey matters, and your stories count!

> *"The most important story we'll ever write in life is our own – not with ink, but with our daily choices."*
> —RICHARD PAUL EVANS

ROADMAP TO GET STARTED

This **5-Step Plan of Action** will help you find your rhythm and gain momentum as you begin this 90-day journey to optimize your mental performance.

1. Day One: Read the **Performance Results Record** introduction, page 19 – 21.
2. Day One: Read and complete your first day of the **Daily Performance Journal Pages**, pages 25 – 31.
3. Day One: Read and complete **Things I Can Control vs Things I Cannot Control Drill**, pages 227 - 229.
4. Day Two: Complete your second day of the **Daily Performance Journal Pages**, page 32 – 33.
5. Day Two: Review the other **Mental Performance Drills**, pages 231 – 321, and choose a drill to work on that sparks your interest.

For the next 90 days, your process of building your *Championship Playbook* will include daily work of: Completing a set of **Daily Performance Journaling Pages** and working on a minimum of one **Mental Performance Drill**. Enjoy your journey of becoming the best at getting better, one day at a time.

I have learned unequivocally: No one gets anywhere or accomplishes anything challenging, difficult or worthy, alone. I have found connecting with others; building an elite inner circle, cultivating authentic relationships, asking for help, and stepping up to help others shifted my mindset and transformed my life. I encourage you to give a copy of this book to someone who is on a similar journey as you and work this process together. Holding each other accountable, providing each other with support and encouragement will produce an extreme edge that you both will have earned. This extreme edge is precisely what optimizes growth.

> *"Striving together we can all get better."*
> —DONENE TAYLOR

Your mission in doing this work is to build your playbook of how to rundown your Bold Goals, at an **OPTIMAL LEVEL.** Should you want to dive deeper into mental performance strategies, you may want to check out my book, *Heart of a Champion*, available on Amazon.

Should you want additional coaching, support, and accountability, it would be my honor to coach you. You can find my contact information in the back of this *Championship Playbook*.

Master the Art of Winning: A Championship Playbook to Optimize Mental Performance gives you the opportunity to dig deeper and do the work necessary to take your next, best step forward, as you rundown your Bold Goals, and that, my friend, is a wild adventure!

I am cheering you on and always rooting for you!

Donene Taylor

PERFORMANCE RESULTS RECORD

*"Compete with yourself.
Compare yourself to no one."*

—DONENE TAYLOR

Performance Results Record

The **Performance Results Record** is a valuable resource that provides you a quick reference to previous competitions and trainings. Use this record to document the date, location, and event. I encourage you to be consistent documenting your results and the page numbers from your completed daily *Master the Art of Winning Performance Journal* pages.

The **Performance Results Record** is helpful as it serves as a reference for:
1. Past successes and wins
2. Past struggles and mistakes
3. When you have made an equipment adjustment or change
4. Different conditions/situations you have performed in
5. Your mindset and mental game while performing
6. Lessons and learns you received while performing
7. Your process and routines

Documenting your result gives you a *benchmark*. This is a tool to help evaluate performance; it is a measurement. The result that you receive from your performance of the competition is packed full of information, data, and feedback.

Your results are absolutely, positively not a measurement of your self-worth. Nor is it a measurement of who you are, what you are capable of, or what you will accomplish. Results are a *benchmark* of your skills in that moment of time. Results are temporary.

The meaning that results have in your life is the meaning that you choose to give it. I want to encourage you to put on your scientist lab coat, unpack the data from your results, and become the best at getting better.

For example, at the competition, when you get the results you have been working towards this is an indicator that your training, and daily habits and routines of excellence may be working. Your result is a *benchmark* of your skill level while competing, at that time.

At the competition, when you do not get the results you have been working towards, this is an indicator that you may want to adjust your training and daily habits and routines. You may need different strategies, invest more time, give more effort. Your result is a *benchmark* of your skill level while competing, at that time.

Champions develop their best by continuous learning, growing, and evolving.

DATE	LOCATION	EVENT	RESULTS	JOURNAL PAGES
August 4th	Troy's Arena	Tie-Down Roping Lesson	I AM READY!!	28 – 29

DATE	LOCATION	EVENT	RESULTS	JOURNAL PAGES

DATE	LOCATION	EVENT	RESULTS	JOURNAL PAGES

PERFORMANCE RESULTS RECORD · **23**

DATE	LOCATION	EVENT	RESULTS	JOURNAL PAGES

DAILY PERFORMANCE JOURNAL PAGES

"Whatever you vividly imagine, ardently desire, sincerely believe, and enthusiastically act upon... must inevitably come to pass!"

—PAUL J. MEYER

Building A Performance Journal

RIDDLE: How do you eat an elephant? Answer: One bite at a time.

I was decades into my journey of running down my Bold Goal of winning a World Championship when I first heard this riddle. As I heard the answer, I smiled and giggled. I was also incredibly sparked! The answer to this riddle was speaking not only to how to eat an elephant but how you do anything and everything in life.

This riddle is all about process. These are a few examples of how we each experience process in the purest form.

- How do you stay alive? One breath at a time.
- How do you think? One thought at a time.
- How do you speak? One word at a time.
- How do you choose? One decision at a time.
- How do you move forward? One step at a time.
- How do you progress? One productive habit at a time.
- How do you rundown Bold Goals? One tiny goal at a time.
- How do you live an amazing life? One day at a time.

The **Daily Performance Journal Pages** will help you establish your process of building your *Championship Playbook* and optimizing your mental performance, one journal page at a time.

You may have asked yourself, *"How will I complete this Championship Playbook?"*

Answer: Journaling one day at a time, for 90 days.

This my friend is process. Living your life moment to moment to moment is how Bold Goals get accomplished. Having a process and working your process is how the impossible becomes possible.

Your process goal of building your *Championship Playbook* is to intentionally press your pause button at the end of each week. Then, reflect and refocus on your past 7 days of journaling pages. I guarantee this will be enlightening.

END OF WEEK REFLECT AND REFOCUS QUESTIONS

The following are some thought-provoking questions you may want to ask yourself as you complete your weekly reflect and refocus review.

1. What are common denominators that I experience during my day that are either helping me or hindering me?
2. What will I STOP doing that will help me take my next, best step forward?
3. What will I START doing that will help me take my next, best step forward?
4. What will I CONTINUE doing that will help me take my next, best step forward?
5. What will I do to be the best at getting better?

Investing time reflecting and refocusing on what you have journaled helps you eliminate making the same mistakes over and over. This process also helps you identify each of your productive and positive actions so you can repeat them. What gets rewarded, gets repeated. What you measure, gets managed.

Each of your completed **Daily Performance Journal Pages** will prove to be a valuable resource. You will use your *Championship Playbook* season after season.

I invite you to review my performance journaling pages. This is a snapshot of one of my training sessions.

Investing time in training yourself to journal about your performance is how you will become better at it. If you are looking for the secret sauce of how to be the best at journaling, here it is:

JUST DO IT!

Building and consistently maintaining your Championship Playbook allows you to have peace when you perform. The peace comes from knowing you are prepared. You will perform optimally, and you will take your next, best step forward – no matter what the results.
— **DONENE TAYLOR**

SHOW AND TELL PAGE

USE THESE SHOW AND TELL PAGES AS A "SPARK" TO OPEN YOUR MIND, CREATE, AND PERFORM OPTIMALLY.

GHP PRINCIPLE: 3 THINGS I AM GRATEFUL FOR TODAY.

1. Blue sky and warm sunshine.
2. My horse - Chester
3. My body - I am healthy and strong.

GHP PRINCIPAL: THE MORE GRATITUDE YOU HAVE, THE HAPPIER YOU BECOME. THE HAPPIER YOU ARE, THE BETTER YOU PERFORM.

NOTABLE DETAILS OF MY TRAINING/COMPETITION. This is my last training session before I travel to a competition. Training with Coach Troy at his arena. Trained outside of my comfort zone.

MY GOAL TODAY IS: Be the best at getting better! Stay focused and locked-in on my target from start to finish. Reel-in my target towards me.

MY CONFIDENCE LEVEL IS: I PERFORM OPTIMALLY AT A 4+/5 CONFIDENCE LEVEL.

1 2 3 (4+) 5
Low ←——————————————→ High

MY INTERNAL PERFORMANCE STATE LEVEL IS: I PERFORM OPTIMALLY AT A 7/8 ENERGY LEVEL.

1 2 3 4 5 6 (7) 8 9 10
Low Energy Level ←——————————————→ High Energy Level

IDENTIFY/DESCRIBE SIGNAL LIGHTS I RECOGNIZED: Green – (Yellow) – Red

I recognized a Yellow Light as I walked into the arena. I was focusing on "what if's." The results I may get from this session.

HOW DID I RELEASE MY YELLOW/RED LIGHTS? I took a couple full, deep breaths. I smiled BIG and clapped my hands. I told myself, "What I learn from today's training is exactly what I need to get better."

REVIEW THE RECOGNIZE SIGNAL LIGHTS DRILL, BEGINNING ON PAGE 231, TO LEARN MORE.

Circle One: (TRAINING DAY) or COMPETITION DAY

BIG OR SMALL CELEBRATE IT ALL!!

WHAT DID I DO WELL TODAY? What Gets Rewarded Gets Repeated.

Recognize and release my Yellow Light before my training session! Stayed on a Green Light for the entire training session! Trained being open-minded and gave full effort! Maintained intense focus on my target and reeled it in towards me each run! Ended training session better than how I started! GROWTH!! Worked my Hourglass Performance Routine 100% of the time!

REVIEW THE BUILDING PERFORMANCE ROUTINES DRILL, BEGINNING ON PAGE 287, TO LEARN MORE.

WHAT CAN I DO BETTER? The Struggle Is Necessary In Order To Learn, Grow, and Evolve.

Maintain a stronger core and stay balanced on my feet and in my seat the entire run.

HOW CAN I DO IT DIFFERENTLY? Keep It Super Simple. Be The Best At Getting Better.

Continue my strength and conditioning program. Vividly visualize engaging my core while staying balanced. Warm-up with focused intention on my core/balance.

TODAY I LEARNED THAT: I am getting faster recognizing my signal lights and better releasing them.

MY PERFORMANCE EVALUATION:

1   2   3   4   5   6   8   (9)   10

Did you notice there is not a #7 on the performance evaluation? You are working to be elite and extraordinary, instead of average and mediocre. Your evaluation may include, but is not limited to: your mindset – your focus – being goal-driven and purposeful – progression of skills – effort given – energy level – emotional regulation – getting outside of your comfort zone – using obstacles as an opportunity to grow – learning from your experience – helping others to get better.

DATE: M   T   W   TH   F   S   S

GHP PRINCIPLE: 3 THINGS I AM GRATEFUL FOR TODAY.

1.

2.

3.

NOTABLE DETAILS OF MY TRAINING/COMPETITION.

MY GOAL TODAY IS:

MY CONFIDENCE LEVEL IS:

Low   1   2   3   4   5   High

MY INTERNAL PERFORMANCE STATE LEVEL IS:

1   2   3   4   5   6   7   8   9   10

Low Energy Level ⟵⟶ High Energy Level

IDENTIFY/DESCRIBE SIGNAL LIGHTS I RECOGNIZED: Green – Yellow – Red

HOW DID I RELEASE MY YELLOW/RED LIGHTS?

Circle One: TRAINING DAY or COMPETITION DAY

WHAT DID I DO WELL TODAY? What Gets Rewarded Gets Repeated.

WHAT CAN I DO BETTER? The Struggle Is Necessary In Order To Learn, Grow, and Evolve.

HOW CAN I DO IT DIFFERENTLY? Keep It Super Simple. Be The Best At Getting Better.

TODAY I LEARNED THAT:

MY PERFORMANCE EVALUATION:

1   2   3   4   5   6   8   9   10

Did you notice there is not a #7 on the performance evaluation? You are working to be elite and extraordinary, instead of average and mediocre. Your evaluation may include, but is not limited to: your mindset – your focus – being goal-driven and purposeful – progression of skills – effort given – energy level – emotional regulation – getting outside of your comfort zone – using obstacles as an opportunity to grow – learning from your experience – helping others to get better.

DATE: M   T   W   TH   F   S   S

GHP PRINCIPLE: 3 THINGS I AM GRATEFUL FOR TODAY.

1.

2.

3.

NOTABLE DETAILS OF MY TRAINING/COMPETITION.

MY GOAL TODAY IS:

MY CONFIDENCE LEVEL IS:

Low   1   2   3   4   5   High

MY INTERNAL PERFORMANCE STATE LEVEL IS:

1   2   3   4   5   6   7   8   9   10
Low Energy Level ←——————————————→ High Energy Level

IDENTIFY/DESCRIBE SIGNAL LIGHTS I RECOGNIZED: Green – Yellow – Red

HOW DID I RELEASE MY YELLOW/RED LIGHTS?

Circle One: TRAINING DAY or COMPETITION DAY

WHAT DID I DO WELL TODAY? What Gets Rewarded Gets Repeated.

WHAT CAN I DO BETTER? The Struggle Is Necessary In Order To Learn, Grow, and Evolve.

HOW CAN I DO IT DIFFERENTLY? Keep It Super Simple. Be The Best At Getting Better.

TODAY I LEARNED THAT:

MY PERFORMANCE EVALUATION:

1   2   3   4   5   6   8   9   10

Did you notice there is not a #7 on the performance evaluation? You are working to be elite and extraordinary, instead of average and mediocre. Your evaluation may include, but is not limited to: your mindset – your focus – being goal-driven and purposeful – progression of skills – effort given – energy level – emotional regulation – getting outside of your comfort zone – using obstacles as an opportunity to grow – learning from your experience – helping others to get better.

DAILY PERFORMANCE JOURNAL PAGES • 33

DATE: M   T   W   TH   F   S   S

GHP PRINCIPLE: 3 THINGS I AM GRATEFUL FOR TODAY.

1.

2.

3.

NOTABLE DETAILS OF MY TRAINING/COMPETITION.

MY GOAL TODAY IS:

MY CONFIDENCE LEVEL IS:

Low 1 ←―――― 2 ―――― 3 ―――― 4 ―――― 5 → High

MY INTERNAL PERFORMANCE STATE LEVEL IS:

1   2   3   4   5   6   7   8   9   10
Low Energy Level ←――――――――――→ High Energy Level

IDENTIFY/DESCRIBE SIGNAL LIGHTS I RECOGNIZED: Green – Yellow – Red

HOW DID I RELEASE MY YELLOW/RED LIGHTS?

Circle One: TRAINING DAY or COMPETITION DAY

WHAT DID I DO WELL TODAY? What Gets Rewarded Gets Repeated.

WHAT CAN I DO BETTER? The Struggle Is Necessary In Order To Learn, Grow, and Evolve.

HOW CAN I DO IT DIFFERENTLY? Keep It Super Simple. Be The Best At Getting Better.

TODAY I LEARNED THAT:

MY PERFORMANCE EVALUATION:

1   2   3   4   5   6   8   9   10

Did you notice there is not a #7 on the performance evaluation? You are working to be elite and extraordinary, instead of average and mediocre. Your evaluation may include, but is not limited to: your mindset – your focus – being goal-driven and purposeful – progression of skills – effort given – energy level – emotional regulation – getting outside of your comfort zone – using obstacles as an opportunity to grow – learning from your experience – helping others to get better.

DATE: M   T   W   TH   F   S   S

GHP PRINCIPLE: 3 THINGS I AM GRATEFUL FOR TODAY.

1.
2.
3.

NOTABLE DETAILS OF MY TRAINING/COMPETITION.

MY GOAL TODAY IS:

MY CONFIDENCE LEVEL IS:

Low   1   2   3   4   5   High

MY INTERNAL PERFORMANCE STATE LEVEL IS:

1   2   3   4   5   6   7   8   9   10

Low Energy Level ⟵⟶ High Energy Level

IDENTIFY/DESCRIBE SIGNAL LIGHTS I RECOGNIZED: Green – Yellow – Red

HOW DID I RELEASE MY YELLOW/RED LIGHTS?

36 • MASTER THE ART OF WINNING

Circle One: TRAINING DAY or COMPETITION DAY

WHAT DID I DO WELL TODAY? What Gets Rewarded Gets Repeated.

WHAT CAN I DO BETTER? The Struggle Is Necessary In Order To Learn, Grow, and Evolve.

HOW CAN I DO IT DIFFERENTLY? Keep It Super Simple. Be The Best At Getting Better.

TODAY I LEARNED THAT:

MY PERFORMANCE EVALUATION:

1   2   3   4   5   6   8   9   10

Did you notice there is not a #7 on the performance evaluation? You are working to be elite and extraordinary, instead of average and mediocre. Your evaluation may include, but is not limited to: your mindset – your focus – being goal-driven and purposeful – progression of skills – effort given – energy level – emotional regulation – getting outside of your comfort zone – using obstacles as an opportunity to grow – learning from your experience – helping others to get better.

DATE: M   T   W   TH   F   S   S

GHP PRINCIPLE: 3 THINGS I AM GRATEFUL FOR TODAY.

1.

2.

3.

NOTABLE DETAILS OF MY TRAINING/COMPETITION.

MY GOAL TODAY IS:

MY CONFIDENCE LEVEL IS:

Low   1   2   3   4   5   High

MY INTERNAL PERFORMANCE STATE LEVEL IS:

1   2   3   4   5   6   7   8   9   10

Low Energy Level   High Energy Level

IDENTIFY/DESCRIBE SIGNAL LIGHTS I RECOGNIZED: Green – Yellow – Red

HOW DID I RELEASE MY YELLOW/RED LIGHTS?

Circle One: TRAINING DAY or COMPETITION DAY

WHAT DID I DO <u>WELL</u> TODAY? What Gets Rewarded Gets Repeated.

WHAT CAN I DO <u>BETTER</u>? The Struggle Is Necessary In Order To Learn, Grow, and Evolve.

<u>HOW</u> CAN I DO IT DIFFERENTLY? Keep It Super Simple. Be The Best At Getting Better.

TODAY I LEARNED THAT:

MY PERFORMANCE EVALUATION:

1   2   3   4   5   6   8   9   10

Did you notice there is not a #7 on the performance evaluation? You are working to be elite and extraordinary, instead of average and mediocre. Your evaluation may include, but is not limited to: your mindset – your focus – being goal-driven and purposeful – progression of skills – effort given – energy level – emotional regulation – getting outside of your comfort zone – using obstacles as an opportunity to grow – learning from your experience – helping others to get better.

DATE: .... M T W TH F S S

GHP PRINCIPLE: 3 THINGS I AM GRATEFUL FOR TODAY.

1.
2.
3.

NOTABLE DETAILS OF MY TRAINING/COMPETITION.

MY GOAL TODAY IS:

MY CONFIDENCE LEVEL IS:

Low   1   2   3   4   5   High

MY INTERNAL PERFORMANCE STATE LEVEL IS:

1 2 3 4 5 6 7 8 9 10
Low Energy Level ←————————————→ High Energy Level

IDENTIFY/DESCRIBE SIGNAL LIGHTS I RECOGNIZED: Green – Yellow – Red

HOW DID I RELEASE MY YELLOW/RED LIGHTS?

Circle One: TRAINING DAY or COMPETITION DAY

WHAT DID I DO WELL TODAY? What Gets Rewarded Gets Repeated.

WHAT CAN I DO BETTER? The Struggle Is Necessary In Order To Learn, Grow, and Evolve.

HOW CAN I DO IT DIFFERENTLY? Keep It Super Simple. Be The Best At Getting Better.

TODAY I LEARNED THAT:

MY PERFORMANCE EVALUATION:

1   2   3   4   5   6   8   9   10

Did you notice there is not a #7 on the performance evaluation? You are working to be elite and extraordinary, instead of average and mediocre. Your evaluation may include, but is not limited to: your mindset – your focus – being goal-driven and purposeful – progression of skills – effort given – energy level – emotional regulation – getting outside of your comfort zone – using obstacles as an opportunity to grow – learning from your experience – helping others to get better.

DATE: .... M   T   W   TH   F   S   S

GHP PRINCIPLE: 3 THINGS I AM GRATEFUL FOR TODAY.

1.
2.
3.

NOTABLE DETAILS OF MY TRAINING/COMPETITION.

MY GOAL TODAY IS:

MY CONFIDENCE LEVEL IS:

```
        1           2           3           4           5
Low  ←                                                      →  High
```

MY INTERNAL PERFORMANCE STATE LEVEL IS:

```
1    2    3    4    5    6    7    8    9    10
Low Energy Level  ←                    →  High Energy Level
```

IDENTIFY/DESCRIBE SIGNAL LIGHTS I RECOGNIZED: Green – Yellow – Red

HOW DID I RELEASE MY YELLOW/RED LIGHTS?

Circle One: TRAINING DAY or COMPETITION DAY

WHAT DID I DO WELL TODAY? What Gets Rewarded Gets Repeated.

WHAT CAN I DO BETTER? The Struggle Is Necessary In Order To Learn, Grow, and Evolve.

HOW CAN I DO IT DIFFERENTLY? Keep It Super Simple. Be The Best At Getting Better.

TODAY I LEARNED THAT:

MY PERFORMANCE EVALUATION:

1   2   3   4   5   6   8   9   10

Did you notice there is not a #7 on the performance evaluation? You are working to be elite and extraordinary, instead of average and mediocre. Your evaluation may include, but is not limited to: your mindset – your focus – being goal-driven and purposeful – progression of skills – effort given – energy level – emotional regulation – getting outside of your comfort zone – using obstacles as an opportunity to grow – learning from your experience – helping others to get better.

DATE: M   T   W   TH   F   S   S

GHP PRINCIPLE: 3 THINGS I AM GRATEFUL FOR TODAY.

1.
2.
3.

NOTABLE DETAILS OF MY TRAINING/COMPETITION.

MY GOAL TODAY IS:

MY CONFIDENCE LEVEL IS:

Low   1   2   3   4   5   High

MY INTERNAL PERFORMANCE STATE LEVEL IS:

1   2   3   4   5   6   7   8   9   10

Low Energy Level ⟵⟶ High Energy Level

IDENTIFY/DESCRIBE SIGNAL LIGHTS I RECOGNIZED: Green – Yellow – Red

HOW DID I RELEASE MY YELLOW/RED LIGHTS?

Circle One: TRAINING DAY or COMPETITION DAY

WHAT DID I DO WELL TODAY? What Gets Rewarded Gets Repeated.

WHAT CAN I DO BETTER? The Struggle Is Necessary In Order To Learn, Grow, and Evolve.

HOW CAN I DO IT DIFFERENTLY? Keep It Super Simple. Be The Best At Getting Better.

TODAY I LEARNED THAT:

MY PERFORMANCE EVALUATION:

1   2   3   4   5   6   8   9   10

Did you notice there is not a #7 on the performance evaluation? You are working to be elite and extraordinary, instead of average and mediocre. Your evaluation may include, but is not limited to: your mindset – your focus – being goal-driven and purposeful – progression of skills – effort given – energy level – emotional regulation – getting outside of your comfort zone – using obstacles as an opportunity to grow – learning from your experience – helping others to get better.

DATE: .... M   T   W   TH   F   S   S

GHP PRINCIPLE: 3 THINGS I AM GRATEFUL FOR TODAY.

1.
2.
3.

NOTABLE DETAILS OF MY TRAINING/COMPETITION.

MY GOAL TODAY IS:

MY CONFIDENCE LEVEL IS:

Low 1 —— 2 —— 3 —— 4 —— 5 High

MY INTERNAL PERFORMANCE STATE LEVEL IS:

1   2   3   4   5   6   7   8   9   10
Low Energy Level ←————————————→ High Energy Level

IDENTIFY/DESCRIBE SIGNAL LIGHTS I RECOGNIZED: Green – Yellow – Red

HOW DID I RELEASE MY YELLOW/RED LIGHTS?

Circle One: TRAINING DAY or COMPETITION DAY

WHAT DID I DO WELL TODAY? What Gets Rewarded Gets Repeated.

WHAT CAN I DO BETTER? The Struggle Is Necessary In Order To Learn, Grow, and Evolve.

HOW CAN I DO IT DIFFERENTLY? Keep It Super Simple. Be The Best At Getting Better.

TODAY I LEARNED THAT:

MY PERFORMANCE EVALUATION:

1   2   3   4   5   6   8   9   10

Did you notice there is not a #7 on the performance evaluation? You are working to be elite and extraordinary, instead of average and mediocre. Your evaluation may include, but is not limited to: your mindset – your focus – being goal-driven and purposeful – progression of skills – effort given – energy level – emotional regulation – getting outside of your comfort zone – using obstacles as an opportunity to grow – learning from your experience – helping others to get better.

DAILY PERFORMANCE JOURNAL PAGES • 47

DATE: .... M   T   W   TH   F   S   S

GHP PRINCIPLE: 3 THINGS I AM GRATEFUL FOR TODAY.

1.
2.
3.

NOTABLE DETAILS OF MY TRAINING/COMPETITION.

MY GOAL TODAY IS:

MY CONFIDENCE LEVEL IS:

Low   1   2   3   4   5   High

MY INTERNAL PERFORMANCE STATE LEVEL IS:

1   2   3   4   5   6   7   8   9   10
Low Energy Level ←————————————————→ High Energy Level

IDENTIFY/DESCRIBE SIGNAL LIGHTS I RECOGNIZED: Green – Yellow – Red

HOW DID I RELEASE MY YELLOW/RED LIGHTS?

Circle One: TRAINING DAY or COMPETITION DAY

WHAT DID I DO WELL TODAY? What Gets Rewarded Gets Repeated.

WHAT CAN I DO BETTER? The Struggle Is Necessary In Order To Learn, Grow, and Evolve.

HOW CAN I DO IT DIFFERENTLY? Keep It Super Simple. Be The Best At Getting Better.

TODAY I LEARNED THAT:

MY PERFORMANCE EVALUATION:

1   2   3   4   5   6   8   9   10

Did you notice there is not a #7 on the performance evaluation? You are working to be elite and extraordinary, instead of average and mediocre. Your evaluation may include, but is not limited to: your mindset – your focus – being goal-driven and purposeful – progression of skills – effort given – energy level – emotional regulation – getting outside of your comfort zone – using obstacles as an opportunity to grow – learning from your experience – helping others to get better.

DAILY PERFORMANCE JOURNAL PAGES • **49**

DATE: M T W TH F S S

GHP PRINCIPLE: 3 THINGS I AM GRATEFUL FOR TODAY.

1.

2.

3.

NOTABLE DETAILS OF MY TRAINING/COMPETITION.

MY GOAL TODAY IS:

MY CONFIDENCE LEVEL IS:

Low 1 2 3 4 5 High

MY INTERNAL PERFORMANCE STATE LEVEL IS:

1 2 3 4 5 6 7 8 9 10
Low Energy Level ← → High Energy Level

IDENTIFY/DESCRIBE SIGNAL LIGHTS I RECOGNIZED: Green – Yellow – Red

HOW DID I RELEASE MY YELLOW/RED LIGHTS?

Circle One: TRAINING DAY or COMPETITION DAY

WHAT DID I DO WELL TODAY? What Gets Rewarded Gets Repeated.

WHAT CAN I DO BETTER? The Struggle Is Necessary In Order To Learn, Grow, and Evolve.

HOW CAN I DO IT DIFFERENTLY? Keep It Super Simple. Be The Best At Getting Better.

TODAY I LEARNED THAT:

MY PERFORMANCE EVALUATION:

1   2   3   4   5   6   8   9   10

Did you notice there is not a #7 on the performance evaluation? You are working to be elite and extraordinary, instead of average and mediocre. Your evaluation may include, but is not limited to: your mindset – your focus – being goal-driven and purposeful – progression of skills – effort given – energy level – emotional regulation – getting outside of your comfort zone – using obstacles as an opportunity to grow – learning from your experience – helping others to get better.

DAILY PERFORMANCE JOURNAL PAGES • 51

DATE: M   T   W   TH   F   S   S

GHP PRINCIPLE: 3 THINGS I AM GRATEFUL FOR TODAY.

1.

2.

3.

NOTABLE DETAILS OF MY TRAINING/COMPETITION.

MY GOAL TODAY IS:

MY CONFIDENCE LEVEL IS:

Low   1   2   3   4   5   High

MY INTERNAL PERFORMANCE STATE LEVEL IS:

1   2   3   4   5   6   7   8   9   10
Low Energy Level ⟵————————⟶ High Energy Level

IDENTIFY/DESCRIBE SIGNAL LIGHTS I RECOGNIZED: Green – Yellow – Red

HOW DID I RELEASE MY YELLOW/RED LIGHTS?

Circle One: TRAINING DAY or COMPETITION DAY

WHAT DID I DO WELL TODAY? What Gets Rewarded Gets Repeated.

WHAT CAN I DO BETTER? The Struggle Is Necessary In Order To Learn, Grow, and Evolve.

HOW CAN I DO IT DIFFERENTLY? Keep It Super Simple. Be The Best At Getting Better.

TODAY I LEARNED THAT:

MY PERFORMANCE EVALUATION:

1   2   3   4   5   6   8   9   10

Did you notice there is not a #7 on the performance evaluation? You are working to be elite and extraordinary, instead of average and mediocre. Your evaluation may include, but is not limited to: your mindset – your focus – being goal-driven and purposeful – progression of skills – effort given – energy level – emotional regulation – getting outside of your comfort zone – using obstacles as an opportunity to grow – learning from your experience – helping others to get better.

DATE: M   T   W   TH   F   S   S

GHP PRINCIPLE: 3 THINGS I AM GRATEFUL FOR TODAY.

1.

2.

3.

NOTABLE DETAILS OF MY TRAINING/COMPETITION.

MY GOAL TODAY IS:

MY CONFIDENCE LEVEL IS:

Low ← 1   2   3   4   5 → High

MY INTERNAL PERFORMANCE STATE LEVEL IS:

1   2   3   4   5   6   7   8   9   10

Low Energy Level ←————————→ High Energy Level

IDENTIFY/DESCRIBE SIGNAL LIGHTS I RECOGNIZED: Green – Yellow – Red

HOW DID I RELEASE MY YELLOW/RED LIGHTS?

Circle One: TRAINING DAY or COMPETITION DAY

WHAT DID I DO WELL TODAY? What Gets Rewarded Gets Repeated.

WHAT CAN I DO BETTER? The Struggle Is Necessary In Order To Learn, Grow, and Evolve.

HOW CAN I DO IT DIFFERENTLY? Keep It Super Simple. Be The Best At Getting Better.

TODAY I LEARNED THAT:

MY PERFORMANCE EVALUATION:

1   2   3   4   5   6   8   9   10

Did you notice there is not a #7 on the performance evaluation? You are working to be elite and extraordinary, instead of average and mediocre. Your evaluation may include, but is not limited to: your mindset – your focus – being goal-driven and purposeful – progression of skills – effort given – energy level – emotional regulation – getting outside of your comfort zone – using obstacles as an opportunity to grow – learning from your experience – helping others to get better.

DAILY PERFORMANCE JOURNAL PAGES • **55**

DATE: M   T   W   TH   F   S   S

GHP PRINCIPLE: 3 THINGS I AM GRATEFUL FOR TODAY.

1.
2.
3.

NOTABLE DETAILS OF MY TRAINING/COMPETITION.

MY GOAL TODAY IS:

MY CONFIDENCE LEVEL IS:

        1   2   3   4   5
Low ⟵————————————————⟶ High

MY INTERNAL PERFORMANCE STATE LEVEL IS:

1   2   3   4   5   6   7   8   9   10
Low Energy Level ⟵————————⟶ High Energy Level

IDENTIFY/DESCRIBE SIGNAL LIGHTS I RECOGNIZED: Green – Yellow – Red

HOW DID I RELEASE MY YELLOW/RED LIGHTS?

Circle One: TRAINING DAY or COMPETITION DAY

WHAT DID I DO WELL TODAY? What Gets Rewarded Gets Repeated.

WHAT CAN I DO BETTER? The Struggle Is Necessary In Order To Learn, Grow, and Evolve.

HOW CAN I DO IT DIFFERENTLY? Keep It Super Simple. Be The Best At Getting Better.

TODAY I LEARNED THAT:

MY PERFORMANCE EVALUATION:

1   2   3   4   5   6   8   9   10

Did you notice there is not a #7 on the performance evaluation? You are working to be elite and extraordinary, instead of average and mediocre. Your evaluation may include, but is not limited to: your mindset – your focus – being goal-driven and purposeful – progression of skills – effort given – energy level – emotional regulation – getting outside of your comfort zone – using obstacles as an opportunity to grow – learning from your experience – helping others to get better.

DATE: M   T   W   TH   F   S   S

GHP PRINCIPLE: 3 THINGS I AM GRATEFUL FOR TODAY.

1.

2.

3.

NOTABLE DETAILS OF MY TRAINING/COMPETITION.

MY GOAL TODAY IS:

MY CONFIDENCE LEVEL IS:

Low 1   2   3   4   5 High

MY INTERNAL PERFORMANCE STATE LEVEL IS:

1 2 3 4 5 6 7 8 9 10

Low Energy Level ⟵⟶ High Energy Level

IDENTIFY/DESCRIBE SIGNAL LIGHTS I RECOGNIZED: Green – Yellow – Red

HOW DID I RELEASE MY YELLOW/RED LIGHTS?

Circle One: TRAINING DAY or COMPETITION DAY

WHAT DID I DO WELL TODAY? What Gets Rewarded Gets Repeated.

WHAT CAN I DO BETTER? The Struggle Is Necessary In Order To Learn, Grow, and Evolve.

HOW CAN I DO IT DIFFERENTLY? Keep It Super Simple. Be The Best At Getting Better.

TODAY I LEARNED THAT:

MY PERFORMANCE EVALUATION:

1   2   3   4   5   6   8   9   10

Did you notice there is not a #7 on the performance evaluation? You are working to be elite and extraordinary, instead of average and mediocre. Your evaluation may include, but is not limited to: your mindset – your focus – being goal-driven and purposeful – progression of skills – effort given – energy level – emotional regulation – getting outside of your comfort zone – using obstacles as an opportunity to grow – learning from your experience – helping others to get better.

DATE: M   T   W   TH   F   S   S

GHP PRINCIPLE: 3 THINGS I AM GRATEFUL FOR TODAY.

1.

2.

3.

NOTABLE DETAILS OF MY TRAINING/COMPETITION.

MY GOAL TODAY IS:

MY CONFIDENCE LEVEL IS:

```
        1              2              3              4              5
Low ←                                                                    → High
```

MY INTERNAL PERFORMANCE STATE LEVEL IS:

```
1    2    3    4    5    6    7    8    9    10
Low Energy Level  ←                    →   High Energy Level
```

IDENTIFY/DESCRIBE SIGNAL LIGHTS I RECOGNIZED: Green – Yellow – Red

HOW DID I RELEASE MY YELLOW/RED LIGHTS?

Circle One: TRAINING DAY or COMPETITION DAY

WHAT DID I DO WELL TODAY? What Gets Rewarded Gets Repeated.

WHAT CAN I DO BETTER? The Struggle Is Necessary In Order To Learn, Grow, and Evolve.

HOW CAN I DO IT DIFFERENTLY? Keep It Super Simple. Be The Best At Getting Better.

TODAY I LEARNED THAT:

MY PERFORMANCE EVALUATION:

1   2   3   4   5   6   8   9   10

Did you notice there is not a #7 on the performance evaluation? You are working to be elite and extraordinary, instead of average and mediocre. Your evaluation may include, but is not limited to: your mindset – your focus – being goal-driven and purposeful – progression of skills – effort given – energy level – emotional regulation – getting outside of your comfort zone – using obstacles as an opportunity to grow – learning from your experience – helping others to get better.

DATE: M   T   W   TH   F   S   S

GHP PRINCIPLE: 3 THINGS I AM GRATEFUL FOR TODAY.

1.

2.

3.

NOTABLE DETAILS OF MY TRAINING/COMPETITION.

MY GOAL TODAY IS:

MY CONFIDENCE LEVEL IS:

        1   2   3   4   5
Low ←——————————————————————→ High

MY INTERNAL PERFORMANCE STATE LEVEL IS:

1   2   3   4   5   6   7   8   9   10
Low Energy Level ←——————————————→ High Energy Level

IDENTIFY/DESCRIBE SIGNAL LIGHTS I RECOGNIZED: Green – Yellow – Red

HOW DID I RELEASE MY YELLOW/RED LIGHTS?

Circle One: TRAINING DAY or COMPETITION DAY

WHAT DID I DO WELL TODAY? What Gets Rewarded Gets Repeated.

WHAT CAN I DO BETTER? The Struggle Is Necessary In Order To Learn, Grow, and Evolve.

HOW CAN I DO IT DIFFERENTLY? Keep It Super Simple. Be The Best At Getting Better.

TODAY I LEARNED THAT:

MY PERFORMANCE EVALUATION:

1   2   3   4   5   6   8   9   10

Did you notice there is not a #7 on the performance evaluation? You are working to be elite and extraordinary, instead of average and mediocre. Your evaluation may include, but is not limited to: your mindset – your focus – being goal-driven and purposeful – progression of skills – effort given – energy level – emotional regulation – getting outside of your comfort zone – using obstacles as an opportunity to grow – learning from your experience – helping others to get better.

DATE: M   T   W   TH   F   S   S

GHP PRINCIPLE: 3 THINGS I AM GRATEFUL FOR TODAY.

1.
2.
3.

NOTABLE DETAILS OF MY TRAINING/COMPETITION.

MY GOAL TODAY IS:

MY CONFIDENCE LEVEL IS:

Low   1   2   3   4   5   High

MY INTERNAL PERFORMANCE STATE LEVEL IS:

1   2   3   4   5   6   7   8   9   10

Low Energy Level ←————————————→ High Energy Level

IDENTIFY/DESCRIBE SIGNAL LIGHTS I RECOGNIZED: Green – Yellow – Red

HOW DID I RELEASE MY YELLOW/RED LIGHTS?

Circle One: TRAINING DAY or COMPETITION DAY

WHAT DID I DO WELL TODAY? What Gets Rewarded Gets Repeated.

WHAT CAN I DO BETTER? The Struggle Is Necessary In Order To Learn, Grow, and Evolve.

HOW CAN I DO IT DIFFERENTLY? Keep It Super Simple. Be The Best At Getting Better.

TODAY I LEARNED THAT:

MY PERFORMANCE EVALUATION:

1   2   3   4   5   6   8   9   10

Did you notice there is not a #7 on the performance evaluation? You are working to be elite and extraordinary, instead of average and mediocre. Your evaluation may include, but is not limited to: your mindset – your focus – being goal-driven and purposeful – progression of skills – effort given – energy level – emotional regulation – getting outside of your comfort zone – using obstacles as an opportunity to grow – learning from your experience – helping others to get better.

DAILY PERFORMANCE JOURNAL PAGES • **65**

DATE: M   T   W   TH   F   S   S

GHP PRINCIPLE: 3 THINGS I AM GRATEFUL FOR TODAY.

1.

2.

3.

NOTABLE DETAILS OF MY TRAINING/COMPETITION.

MY GOAL TODAY IS:

MY CONFIDENCE LEVEL IS:

     1   2   3   4   5
Low ⟵——————————————————⟶ High

MY INTERNAL PERFORMANCE STATE LEVEL IS:

1   2   3   4   5   6   7   8   9   10
Low Energy Level ⟵——————————⟶ High Energy Level

IDENTIFY/DESCRIBE SIGNAL LIGHTS I RECOGNIZED: Green – Yellow – Red

HOW DID I RELEASE MY YELLOW/RED LIGHTS?

Circle One: TRAINING DAY or COMPETITION DAY

WHAT DID I DO <u>WELL</u> TODAY? What Gets Rewarded Gets Repeated.

WHAT CAN I DO <u>BETTER</u>? The Struggle Is Necessary In Order To Learn, Grow, and Evolve.

<u>HOW</u> CAN I DO IT DIFFERENTLY? Keep It Super Simple. Be The Best At Getting Better.

TODAY I LEARNED THAT:

MY PERFORMANCE EVALUATION:

1   2   3   4   5   6   8   9   10

Did you notice there is not a #7 on the performance evaluation? You are working to be elite and extraordinary, instead of average and mediocre. Your evaluation may include, but is not limited to: your mindset – your focus – being goal-driven and purposeful – progression of skills – effort given – energy level – emotional regulation – getting outside of your comfort zone – using obstacles as an opportunity to grow – learning from your experience – helping others to get better.

DAILY PERFORMANCE JOURNAL PAGES • **67**

DATE: M   T   W   TH   F   S   S

GHP PRINCIPLE: 3 THINGS I AM GRATEFUL FOR TODAY.

1.

2.

3.

NOTABLE DETAILS OF MY TRAINING/COMPETITION.

MY GOAL TODAY IS:

MY CONFIDENCE LEVEL IS:

```
         1              2              3              4              5
Low ←                                                                    → High
```

MY INTERNAL PERFORMANCE STATE LEVEL IS:

```
1     2     3     4     5     6     7     8     9     10
Low Energy Level ←                              → High Energy Level
```

IDENTIFY/DESCRIBE SIGNAL LIGHTS I RECOGNIZED: Green – Yellow – Red

HOW DID I RELEASE MY YELLOW/RED LIGHTS?

Circle One: TRAINING DAY or COMPETITION DAY

WHAT DID I DO WELL TODAY? What Gets Rewarded Gets Repeated.

WHAT CAN I DO BETTER? The Struggle Is Necessary In Order To Learn, Grow, and Evolve.

HOW CAN I DO IT DIFFERENTLY? Keep It Super Simple. Be The Best At Getting Better.

TODAY I LEARNED THAT:

MY PERFORMANCE EVALUATION:

1   2   3   4   5   6   8   9   10

Did you notice there is not a #7 on the performance evaluation? You are working to be elite and extraordinary, instead of average and mediocre. Your evaluation may include, but is not limited to: your mindset – your focus – being goal-driven and purposeful – progression of skills – effort given – energy level – emotional regulation – getting outside of your comfort zone – using obstacles as an opportunity to grow – learning from your experience – helping others to get better.

DATE: M   T   W   TH   F   S   S

GHP PRINCIPLE: 3 THINGS I AM GRATEFUL FOR TODAY.

1.

2.

3.

NOTABLE DETAILS OF MY TRAINING/COMPETITION.

MY GOAL TODAY IS:

MY CONFIDENCE LEVEL IS:

Low   1   2   3   4   5   High

MY INTERNAL PERFORMANCE STATE LEVEL IS:

1   2   3   4   5   6   7   8   9   10

Low Energy Level   ⟵⟶   High Energy Level

IDENTIFY/DESCRIBE SIGNAL LIGHTS I RECOGNIZED: Green – Yellow – Red

HOW DID I RELEASE MY YELLOW/RED LIGHTS?

Circle One: TRAINING DAY or COMPETITION DAY

WHAT DID I DO <u>WELL</u> TODAY? What Gets Rewarded Gets Repeated.

WHAT CAN I DO <u>BETTER</u>? The Struggle Is Necessary In Order To Learn, Grow, and Evolve.

<u>HOW</u> CAN I DO IT DIFFERENTLY? Keep It Super Simple. Be The Best At Getting Better.

TODAY I LEARNED THAT:

MY PERFORMANCE EVALUATION:

1   2   3   4   5   6   8   9   10

Did you notice there is not a #7 on the performance evaluation? You are working to be elite and extraordinary, instead of average and mediocre. Your evaluation may include, but is not limited to: your mindset – your focus – being goal-driven and purposeful – progression of skills – effort given – energy level – emotional regulation – getting outside of your comfort zone – using obstacles as an opportunity to grow – learning from your experience – helping others to get better.

DAILY PERFORMANCE JOURNAL PAGES • **71**

DATE: .... M T W TH F S S

GHP PRINCIPLE: 3 THINGS I AM GRATEFUL FOR TODAY.

1.

2.

3.

NOTABLE DETAILS OF MY TRAINING/COMPETITION.

MY GOAL TODAY IS:

MY CONFIDENCE LEVEL IS:

Low 1   2   3   4   5 High

MY INTERNAL PERFORMANCE STATE LEVEL IS:

1 2 3 4 5 6 7 8 9 10
Low Energy Level ←——————————→ High Energy Level

IDENTIFY/DESCRIBE SIGNAL LIGHTS I RECOGNIZED: Green – Yellow – Red

HOW DID I RELEASE MY YELLOW/RED LIGHTS?

Circle One: TRAINING DAY or COMPETITION DAY

WHAT DID I DO WELL TODAY? What Gets Rewarded Gets Repeated.

WHAT CAN I DO BETTER? The Struggle Is Necessary In Order To Learn, Grow, and Evolve.

HOW CAN I DO IT DIFFERENTLY? Keep It Super Simple. Be The Best At Getting Better.

TODAY I LEARNED THAT:

MY PERFORMANCE EVALUATION:

1   2   3   4   5   6   8   9   10

Did you notice there is not a #7 on the performance evaluation? You are working to be elite and extraordinary, instead of average and mediocre. Your evaluation may include, but is not limited to: your mindset – your focus – being goal-driven and purposeful – progression of skills – effort given – energy level – emotional regulation – getting outside of your comfort zone – using obstacles as an opportunity to grow – learning from your experience – helping others to get better.

DATE: M   T   W   TH   F   S   S

GHP PRINCIPLE: 3 THINGS I AM GRATEFUL FOR TODAY.

1.

2.

3.

NOTABLE DETAILS OF MY TRAINING/COMPETITION.

MY GOAL TODAY IS:

MY CONFIDENCE LEVEL IS:

Low   1   2   3   4   5   High

MY INTERNAL PERFORMANCE STATE LEVEL IS:

1   2   3   4   5   6   7   8   9   10

Low Energy Level ⟵⟶ High Energy Level

IDENTIFY/DESCRIBE SIGNAL LIGHTS I RECOGNIZED: Green – Yellow – Red

HOW DID I RELEASE MY YELLOW/RED LIGHTS?

Circle One: TRAINING DAY or COMPETITION DAY

WHAT DID I DO WELL TODAY? What Gets Rewarded Gets Repeated.

WHAT CAN I DO BETTER? The Struggle Is Necessary In Order To Learn, Grow, and Evolve.

HOW CAN I DO IT DIFFERENTLY? Keep It Super Simple. Be The Best At Getting Better.

TODAY I LEARNED THAT:

MY PERFORMANCE EVALUATION:

1   2   3   4   5   6   8   9   10

Did you notice there is not a #7 on the performance evaluation? You are working to be elite and extraordinary, instead of average and mediocre. Your evaluation may include, but is not limited to: your mindset – your focus – being goal-driven and purposeful – progression of skills – effort given – energy level – emotional regulation – getting outside of your comfort zone – using obstacles as an opportunity to grow – learning from your experience – helping others to get better.

DATE: M   T   W   TH   F   S   S

GHP PRINCIPLE: 3 THINGS I AM GRATEFUL FOR TODAY.

1.

2.

3.

NOTABLE DETAILS OF MY TRAINING/COMPETITION.

MY GOAL TODAY IS:

MY CONFIDENCE LEVEL IS:

           1   2   3   4   5
Low ←   → High

MY INTERNAL PERFORMANCE STATE LEVEL IS:

1   2   3   4   5   6   7   8   9   10
Low Energy Level ←   → High Energy Level

IDENTIFY/DESCRIBE SIGNAL LIGHTS I RECOGNIZED: Green – Yellow – Red

HOW DID I RELEASE MY YELLOW/RED LIGHTS?

Circle One: TRAINING DAY or COMPETITION DAY

WHAT DID I DO WELL TODAY? What Gets Rewarded Gets Repeated.

WHAT CAN I DO BETTER? The Struggle Is Necessary In Order To Learn, Grow, and Evolve.

HOW CAN I DO IT DIFFERENTLY? Keep It Super Simple. Be The Best At Getting Better.

TODAY I LEARNED THAT:

MY PERFORMANCE EVALUATION:

1   2   3   4   5   6   8   9   10

Did you notice there is not a #7 on the performance evaluation? You are working to be elite and extraordinary, instead of average and mediocre. Your evaluation may include, but is not limited to: your mindset – your focus – being goal-driven and purposeful – progression of skills – effort given – energy level – emotional regulation – getting outside of your comfort zone – using obstacles as an opportunity to grow – learning from your experience – helping others to get better.

DATE: M   T   W   TH   F   S   S

GHP PRINCIPLE: 3 THINGS I AM GRATEFUL FOR TODAY.

1.

2.

3.

NOTABLE DETAILS OF MY TRAINING/COMPETITION.

MY GOAL TODAY IS:

MY CONFIDENCE LEVEL IS:

Low   1   2   3   4   5   High

MY INTERNAL PERFORMANCE STATE LEVEL IS:

1   2   3   4   5   6   7   8   9   10

Low Energy Level ⟵⟶ High Energy Level

IDENTIFY/DESCRIBE SIGNAL LIGHTS I RECOGNIZED: Green – Yellow – Red

HOW DID I RELEASE MY YELLOW/RED LIGHTS?

Circle One: TRAINING DAY or COMPETITION DAY

WHAT DID I DO WELL TODAY? What Gets Rewarded Gets Repeated.

WHAT CAN I DO BETTER? The Struggle Is Necessary In Order To Learn, Grow, and Evolve.

HOW CAN I DO IT DIFFERENTLY? Keep It Super Simple. Be The Best At Getting Better.

TODAY I LEARNED THAT:

MY PERFORMANCE EVALUATION:

1   2   3   4   5   6   8   9   10

Did you notice there is not a #7 on the performance evaluation? You are working to be elite and extraordinary, instead of average and mediocre. Your evaluation may include, but is not limited to: your mindset – your focus – being goal-driven and purposeful – progression of skills – effort given – energy level – emotional regulation – getting outside of your comfort zone – using obstacles as an opportunity to grow – learning from your experience – helping others to get better.

DATE: M   T   W   TH   F   S   S

GHP PRINCIPLE: 3 THINGS I AM GRATEFUL FOR TODAY.

1.

2.

3.

NOTABLE DETAILS OF MY TRAINING/COMPETITION.

MY GOAL TODAY IS:

MY CONFIDENCE LEVEL IS:

       1   2   3   4   5
Low ⟵⎯⎯⎯⎯⎯⎯⎯⎯⎯⎯⎯⎯⎯⎯⟶ High

MY INTERNAL PERFORMANCE STATE LEVEL IS:

1   2   3   4   5   6   7   8   9   10
Low Energy Level ⟵⎯⎯⎯⎯⎯⎯⎯⎯⟶ High Energy Level

IDENTIFY/DESCRIBE SIGNAL LIGHTS I RECOGNIZED: Green – Yellow – Red

HOW DID I RELEASE MY YELLOW/RED LIGHTS?

Circle One: TRAINING DAY or COMPETITION DAY

WHAT DID I DO WELL TODAY? What Gets Rewarded Gets Repeated.

WHAT CAN I DO BETTER? The Struggle Is Necessary In Order To Learn, Grow, and Evolve.

HOW CAN I DO IT DIFFERENTLY? Keep It Super Simple. Be The Best At Getting Better.

TODAY I LEARNED THAT:

MY PERFORMANCE EVALUATION:

1   2   3   4   5   6   8   9   10

Did you notice there is not a #7 on the performance evaluation? You are working to be elite and extraordinary, instead of average and mediocre. Your evaluation may include, but is not limited to: your mindset – your focus – being goal-driven and purposeful – progression of skills – effort given – energy level – emotional regulation – getting outside of your comfort zone – using obstacles as an opportunity to grow – learning from your experience – helping others to get better.

DATE: M   T   W   TH   F   S   S

GHP PRINCIPLE: 3 THINGS I AM GRATEFUL FOR TODAY.

1.

2.

3.

NOTABLE DETAILS OF MY TRAINING/COMPETITION.

MY GOAL TODAY IS:

MY CONFIDENCE LEVEL IS:

Low   1   2   3   4   5   High

MY INTERNAL PERFORMANCE STATE LEVEL IS:

1   2   3   4   5   6   7   8   9   10

Low Energy Level ⟵⟶ High Energy Level

IDENTIFY/DESCRIBE SIGNAL LIGHTS I RECOGNIZED: Green – Yellow – Red

HOW DID I RELEASE MY YELLOW/RED LIGHTS?

Circle One: TRAINING DAY or COMPETITION DAY

WHAT DID I DO WELL TODAY? What Gets Rewarded Gets Repeated.

WHAT CAN I DO BETTER? The Struggle Is Necessary In Order To Learn, Grow, and Evolve.

HOW CAN I DO IT DIFFERENTLY? Keep It Super Simple. Be The Best At Getting Better.

TODAY I LEARNED THAT:

MY PERFORMANCE EVALUATION:

1   2   3   4   5   6   8   9   10

Did you notice there is not a #7 on the performance evaluation? You are working to be elite and extraordinary, instead of average and mediocre. Your evaluation may include, but is not limited to: your mindset – your focus – being goal-driven and purposeful – progression of skills – effort given – energy level – emotional regulation – getting outside of your comfort zone – using obstacles as an opportunity to grow – learning from your experience – helping others to get better.

DAILY PERFORMANCE JOURNAL PAGES • **83**

DATE: M   T   W   TH   F   S   S

GHP PRINCIPLE: 3 THINGS I AM GRATEFUL FOR TODAY.

1.

2.

3.

NOTABLE DETAILS OF MY TRAINING/COMPETITION.

MY GOAL TODAY IS:

MY CONFIDENCE LEVEL IS:

Low   1   2   3   4   5   High

MY INTERNAL PERFORMANCE STATE LEVEL IS:

1   2   3   4   5   6   7   8   9   10
Low Energy Level ←——————————————→ High Energy Level

IDENTIFY/DESCRIBE SIGNAL LIGHTS I RECOGNIZED: Green – Yellow – Red

HOW DID I RELEASE MY YELLOW/RED LIGHTS?

Circle One: TRAINING DAY or COMPETITION DAY

WHAT DID I DO WELL TODAY? What Gets Rewarded Gets Repeated.

WHAT CAN I DO BETTER? The Struggle Is Necessary In Order To Learn, Grow, and Evolve.

HOW CAN I DO IT DIFFERENTLY? Keep It Super Simple. Be The Best At Getting Better.

TODAY I LEARNED THAT:

MY PERFORMANCE EVALUATION:

1   2   3   4   5   6   8   9   10

Did you notice there is not a #7 on the performance evaluation? You are working to be elite and extraordinary, instead of average and mediocre. Your evaluation may include, but is not limited to: your mindset – your focus – being goal-driven and purposeful – progression of skills – effort given – energy level – emotional regulation – getting outside of your comfort zone – using obstacles as an opportunity to grow – learning from your experience – helping others to get better.

DATE: M   T   W   TH   F   S   S

GHP PRINCIPLE: 3 THINGS I AM GRATEFUL FOR TODAY.

1.

2.

3.

NOTABLE DETAILS OF MY TRAINING/COMPETITION.

MY GOAL TODAY IS:

MY CONFIDENCE LEVEL IS:

Low ← 1   2   3   4   5 → High

MY INTERNAL PERFORMANCE STATE LEVEL IS:

1   2   3   4   5   6   7   8   9   10
Low Energy Level ←————————————————→ High Energy Level

IDENTIFY/DESCRIBE SIGNAL LIGHTS I RECOGNIZED: Green – Yellow – Red

HOW DID I RELEASE MY YELLOW/RED LIGHTS?

Circle One: TRAINING DAY or COMPETITION DAY

WHAT DID I DO WELL TODAY? What Gets Rewarded Gets Repeated.

WHAT CAN I DO BETTER? The Struggle Is Necessary In Order To Learn, Grow, and Evolve.

HOW CAN I DO IT DIFFERENTLY? Keep It Super Simple. Be The Best At Getting Better.

TODAY I LEARNED THAT:

MY PERFORMANCE EVALUATION:

1   2   3   4   5   6   8   9   10

Did you notice there is not a #7 on the performance evaluation? You are working to be elite and extraordinary, instead of average and mediocre. Your evaluation may include, but is not limited to: your mindset – your focus – being goal-driven and purposeful – progression of skills – effort given – energy level – emotional regulation – getting outside of your comfort zone – using obstacles as an opportunity to grow – learning from your experience – helping others to get better.

DATE: M   T   W   TH   F   S   S

GHP PRINCIPLE: 3 THINGS I AM GRATEFUL FOR TODAY.

1.
2.
3.

NOTABLE DETAILS OF MY TRAINING/COMPETITION.

MY GOAL TODAY IS:

MY CONFIDENCE LEVEL IS:

       1   2   3   4   5
Low ⟵——————————————————————⟶ High

MY INTERNAL PERFORMANCE STATE LEVEL IS:

1   2   3   4   5   6   7   8   9   10
Low Energy Level ⟵——————————⟶ High Energy Level

IDENTIFY/DESCRIBE SIGNAL LIGHTS I RECOGNIZED: Green – Yellow – Red

HOW DID I RELEASE MY YELLOW/RED LIGHTS?

Circle One: TRAINING DAY or COMPETITION DAY

WHAT DID I DO WELL TODAY? What Gets Rewarded Gets Repeated.

WHAT CAN I DO BETTER? The Struggle Is Necessary In Order To Learn, Grow, and Evolve.

HOW CAN I DO IT DIFFERENTLY? Keep It Super Simple. Be The Best At Getting Better.

TODAY I LEARNED THAT:

MY PERFORMANCE EVALUATION:

1   2   3   4   5   6   8   9   10

Did you notice there is not a #7 on the performance evaluation? You are working to be elite and extraordinary, instead of average and mediocre. Your evaluation may include, but is not limited to: your mindset – your focus – being goal-driven and purposeful – progression of skills – effort given – energy level – emotional regulation – getting outside of your comfort zone – using obstacles as an opportunity to grow – learning from your experience – helping others to get better.

DATE: _____   M   T   W   TH   F   S   S

GHP PRINCIPLE: 3 THINGS I AM GRATEFUL FOR TODAY.

1.

2.

3.

NOTABLE DETAILS OF MY TRAINING/COMPETITION.

MY GOAL TODAY IS:

MY CONFIDENCE LEVEL IS:

Low ⟵ 1   2   3   4   5 ⟶ High

MY INTERNAL PERFORMANCE STATE LEVEL IS:

1   2   3   4   5   6   7   8   9   10
Low Energy Level ⟵   ⟶ High Energy Level

IDENTIFY/DESCRIBE SIGNAL LIGHTS I RECOGNIZED: Green – Yellow – Red

HOW DID I RELEASE MY YELLOW/RED LIGHTS?

Circle One: TRAINING DAY or COMPETITION DAY

WHAT DID I DO WELL TODAY? What Gets Rewarded Gets Repeated.

WHAT CAN I DO BETTER? The Struggle Is Necessary In Order To Learn, Grow, and Evolve.

HOW CAN I DO IT DIFFERENTLY? Keep It Super Simple. Be The Best At Getting Better.

TODAY I LEARNED THAT:

MY PERFORMANCE EVALUATION:

1   2   3   4   5   6   8   9   10

Did you notice there is not a #7 on the performance evaluation? You are working to be elite and extraordinary, instead of average and mediocre. Your evaluation may include, but is not limited to: your mindset – your focus – being goal-driven and purposeful – progression of skills – effort given – energy level – emotional regulation – getting outside of your comfort zone – using obstacles as an opportunity to grow – learning from your experience – helping others to get better.

DATE: M   T   W   TH   F   S   S

GHP PRINCIPLE: 3 THINGS I AM GRATEFUL FOR TODAY.

1.

2.

3.

NOTABLE DETAILS OF MY TRAINING/COMPETITION.

MY GOAL TODAY IS:

MY CONFIDENCE LEVEL IS:

Low   1   2   3   4   5   High

MY INTERNAL PERFORMANCE STATE LEVEL IS:

1   2   3   4   5   6   7   8   9   10

Low Energy Level ⟵⟶ High Energy Level

IDENTIFY/DESCRIBE SIGNAL LIGHTS I RECOGNIZED: Green – Yellow – Red

HOW DID I RELEASE MY YELLOW/RED LIGHTS?

Circle One: TRAINING DAY or COMPETITION DAY

WHAT DID I DO WELL TODAY? What Gets Rewarded Gets Repeated.

WHAT CAN I DO BETTER? The Struggle Is Necessary In Order To Learn, Grow, and Evolve.

HOW CAN I DO IT DIFFERENTLY? Keep It Super Simple. Be The Best At Getting Better.

TODAY I LEARNED THAT:

MY PERFORMANCE EVALUATION:

1   2   3   4   5   6   8   9   10

Did you notice there is not a #7 on the performance evaluation? You are working to be elite and extraordinary, instead of average and mediocre. Your evaluation may include, but is not limited to: your mindset – your focus – being goal-driven and purposeful – progression of skills – effort given – energy level – emotional regulation – getting outside of your comfort zone – using obstacles as an opportunity to grow – learning from your experience – helping others to get better.

DATE: M   T   W   TH   F   S   S

GHP PRINCIPLE: 3 THINGS I AM GRATEFUL FOR TODAY.

1.

2.

3.

NOTABLE DETAILS OF MY TRAINING/COMPETITION.

MY GOAL TODAY IS:

MY CONFIDENCE LEVEL IS:

Low   1   2   3   4   5   High

MY INTERNAL PERFORMANCE STATE LEVEL IS:

1   2   3   4   5   6   7   8   9   10

Low Energy Level ⟵⟶ High Energy Level

IDENTIFY/DESCRIBE SIGNAL LIGHTS I RECOGNIZED: Green – Yellow – Red

HOW DID I RELEASE MY YELLOW/RED LIGHTS?

Circle One: TRAINING DAY or COMPETITION DAY

WHAT DID I DO WELL TODAY? What Gets Rewarded Gets Repeated.

WHAT CAN I DO BETTER? The Struggle Is Necessary In Order To Learn, Grow, and Evolve.

HOW CAN I DO IT DIFFERENTLY? Keep It Super Simple. Be The Best At Getting Better.

TODAY I LEARNED THAT:

MY PERFORMANCE EVALUATION:

1   2   3   4   5   6   8   9   10

Did you notice there is not a #7 on the performance evaluation? You are working to be elite and extraordinary, instead of average and mediocre. Your evaluation may include, but is not limited to: your mindset – your focus – being goal-driven and purposeful – progression of skills – effort given – energy level – emotional regulation – getting outside of your comfort zone – using obstacles as an opportunity to grow – learning from your experience – helping others to get better.

DATE: M   T   W   TH   F   S   S

GHP PRINCIPLE: 3 THINGS I AM GRATEFUL FOR TODAY.

1.

2.

3.

NOTABLE DETAILS OF MY TRAINING/COMPETITION.

MY GOAL TODAY IS:

MY CONFIDENCE LEVEL IS:

Low   1   2   3   4   5   High

MY INTERNAL PERFORMANCE STATE LEVEL IS:

1   2   3   4   5   6   7   8   9   10

Low Energy Level ⟵⟶ High Energy Level

IDENTIFY/DESCRIBE SIGNAL LIGHTS I RECOGNIZED: Green – Yellow – Red

HOW DID I RELEASE MY YELLOW/RED LIGHTS?

Circle One: TRAINING DAY or COMPETITION DAY

WHAT DID I DO WELL TODAY? What Gets Rewarded Gets Repeated.

WHAT CAN I DO BETTER? The Struggle Is Necessary In Order To Learn, Grow, and Evolve.

HOW CAN I DO IT DIFFERENTLY? Keep It Super Simple. Be The Best At Getting Better.

TODAY I LEARNED THAT:

MY PERFORMANCE EVALUATION:

1   2   3   4   5   6   8   9   10

Did you notice there is not a #7 on the performance evaluation? You are working to be elite and extraordinary, instead of average and mediocre. Your evaluation may include, but is not limited to: your mindset – your focus – being goal-driven and purposeful – progression of skills – effort given – energy level – emotional regulation – getting outside of your comfort zone – using obstacles as an opportunity to grow – learning from your experience – helping others to get better.

DATE: M   T   W   TH   F   S   S

GHP PRINCIPLE: 3 THINGS I AM GRATEFUL FOR TODAY.

1.
2.
3.

NOTABLE DETAILS OF MY TRAINING/COMPETITION.

MY GOAL TODAY IS:

MY CONFIDENCE LEVEL IS:

Low   1   2   3   4   5   High

MY INTERNAL PERFORMANCE STATE LEVEL IS:

1   2   3   4   5   6   7   8   9   10

Low Energy Level ⟵⟶ High Energy Level

IDENTIFY/DESCRIBE SIGNAL LIGHTS I RECOGNIZED: Green – Yellow – Red

HOW DID I RELEASE MY YELLOW/RED LIGHTS?

Circle One: TRAINING DAY or COMPETITION DAY

WHAT DID I DO WELL TODAY? What Gets Rewarded Gets Repeated.

WHAT CAN I DO BETTER? The Struggle Is Necessary In Order To Learn, Grow, and Evolve.

HOW CAN I DO IT DIFFERENTLY? Keep It Super Simple. Be The Best At Getting Better.

TODAY I LEARNED THAT:

MY PERFORMANCE EVALUATION:

1 2 3 4 5 6 8 9 10

Did you notice there is not a #7 on the performance evaluation? You are working to be elite and extraordinary, instead of average and mediocre. Your evaluation may include, but is not limited to: your mindset – your focus – being goal-driven and purposeful – progression of skills – effort given – energy level – emotional regulation – getting outside of your comfort zone – using obstacles as an opportunity to grow – learning from your experience – helping others to get better.

DAILY PERFORMANCE JOURNAL PAGES • **99**

DATE: M   T   W   TH   F   S   S

GHP PRINCIPLE: 3 THINGS I AM GRATEFUL FOR TODAY.

1.
2.
3.

NOTABLE DETAILS OF MY TRAINING/COMPETITION.

MY GOAL TODAY IS:

MY CONFIDENCE LEVEL IS:

Low   1   2   3   4   5   High

MY INTERNAL PERFORMANCE STATE LEVEL IS:

1   2   3   4   5   6   7   8   9   10

Low Energy Level ⟵⟶ High Energy Level

IDENTIFY/DESCRIBE SIGNAL LIGHTS I RECOGNIZED: Green – Yellow – Red

HOW DID I RELEASE MY YELLOW/RED LIGHTS?

Circle One: TRAINING DAY or COMPETITION DAY

WHAT DID I DO WELL TODAY? What Gets Rewarded Gets Repeated.

WHAT CAN I DO BETTER? The Struggle Is Necessary In Order To Learn, Grow, and Evolve.

HOW CAN I DO IT DIFFERENTLY? Keep It Super Simple. Be The Best At Getting Better.

TODAY I LEARNED THAT:

MY PERFORMANCE EVALUATION:

1   2   3   4   5   6   8   9   10

Did you notice there is not a #7 on the performance evaluation? You are working to be elite and extraordinary, instead of average and mediocre. Your evaluation may include, but is not limited to: your mindset – your focus – being goal-driven and purposeful – progression of skills – effort given – energy level – emotional regulation – getting outside of your comfort zone – using obstacles as an opportunity to grow – learning from your experience – helping others to get better.

DATE: M   T   W   TH   F   S   S

GHP PRINCIPLE: 3 THINGS I AM GRATEFUL FOR TODAY.

1.

2.

3.

NOTABLE DETAILS OF MY TRAINING/COMPETITION.

MY GOAL TODAY IS:

MY CONFIDENCE LEVEL IS:

Low   1   2   3   4   5   High

MY INTERNAL PERFORMANCE STATE LEVEL IS:

1   2   3   4   5   6   7   8   9   10

Low Energy Level ⟵⎯⎯⎯⎯⎯⎯⟶ High Energy Level

IDENTIFY/DESCRIBE SIGNAL LIGHTS I RECOGNIZED: Green – Yellow – Red

HOW DID I RELEASE MY YELLOW/RED LIGHTS?

Circle One: TRAINING DAY or COMPETITION DAY

WHAT DID I DO WELL TODAY? What Gets Rewarded Gets Repeated.

WHAT CAN I DO BETTER? The Struggle Is Necessary In Order To Learn, Grow, and Evolve.

HOW CAN I DO IT DIFFERENTLY? Keep It Super Simple. Be The Best At Getting Better.

TODAY I LEARNED THAT:

MY PERFORMANCE EVALUATION:

1   2   3   4   5   6   8   9   10

Did you notice there is not a #7 on the performance evaluation? You are working to be elite and extraordinary, instead of average and mediocre. Your evaluation may include, but is not limited to: your mindset – your focus – being goal-driven and purposeful – progression of skills – effort given – energy level – emotional regulation – getting outside of your comfort zone – using obstacles as an opportunity to grow – learning from your experience – helping others to get better.

DAILY PERFORMANCE JOURNAL PAGES • 103

DATE: _____ M   T   W   TH   F   S   S

GHP PRINCIPLE: 3 THINGS I AM GRATEFUL FOR TODAY.

1.

2.

3.

NOTABLE DETAILS OF MY TRAINING/COMPETITION.

MY GOAL TODAY IS:

MY CONFIDENCE LEVEL IS:

Low   1   2   3   4   5   High

MY INTERNAL PERFORMANCE STATE LEVEL IS:

1   2   3   4   5   6   7   8   9   10

Low Energy Level ⟵⟶ High Energy Level

IDENTIFY/DESCRIBE SIGNAL LIGHTS I RECOGNIZED: Green – Yellow – Red

HOW DID I RELEASE MY YELLOW/RED LIGHTS?

Circle One: TRAINING DAY or COMPETITION DAY

WHAT DID I DO <u>WELL</u> TODAY? What Gets Rewarded Gets Repeated.

WHAT CAN I DO <u>BETTER</u>? The Struggle Is Necessary In Order To Learn, Grow, and Evolve.

<u>HOW</u> CAN I DO IT DIFFERENTLY? Keep It Super Simple. Be The Best At Getting Better.

TODAY I LEARNED THAT:

MY PERFORMANCE EVALUATION:

1 2 3 4 5 6 8 9 10

Did you notice there is not a #7 on the performance evaluation? You are working to be elite and extraordinary, instead of average and mediocre. Your evaluation may include, but is not limited to: your mindset – your focus – being goal-driven and purposeful – progression of skills – effort given – energy level – emotional regulation – getting outside of your comfort zone – using obstacles as an opportunity to grow – learning from your experience – helping others to get better.

DATE: M   T   W   TH   F   S   S

GHP PRINCIPLE: 3 THINGS I AM GRATEFUL FOR TODAY.

1.

2.

3.

NOTABLE DETAILS OF MY TRAINING/COMPETITION.

MY GOAL TODAY IS:

MY CONFIDENCE LEVEL IS:

Low   1   2   3   4   5   High

MY INTERNAL PERFORMANCE STATE LEVEL IS:

1   2   3   4   5   6   7   8   9   10

Low Energy Level ⟵⟶ High Energy Level

IDENTIFY/DESCRIBE SIGNAL LIGHTS I RECOGNIZED: Green – Yellow – Red

HOW DID I RELEASE MY YELLOW/RED LIGHTS?

Circle One: TRAINING DAY or COMPETITION DAY

WHAT DID I DO WELL TODAY? What Gets Rewarded Gets Repeated.

WHAT CAN I DO BETTER? The Struggle Is Necessary In Order To Learn, Grow, and Evolve.

HOW CAN I DO IT DIFFERENTLY? Keep It Super Simple. Be The Best At Getting Better.

TODAY I LEARNED THAT:

MY PERFORMANCE EVALUATION:

1   2   3   4   5   6   8   9   10

Did you notice there is not a #7 on the performance evaluation? You are working to be elite and extraordinary, instead of average and mediocre. Your evaluation may include, but is not limited to: your mindset – your focus – being goal-driven and purposeful – progression of skills – effort given – energy level – emotional regulation – getting outside of your comfort zone – using obstacles as an opportunity to grow – learning from your experience – helping others to get better.

DAILY PERFORMANCE JOURNAL PAGES • **107**

DATE:　　　　　　　　　　　　　　　M　T　W　TH　F　S　S

GHP PRINCIPLE: 3 THINGS I AM GRATEFUL FOR TODAY.

1.
2.
3.

NOTABLE DETAILS OF MY TRAINING/COMPETITION.

MY GOAL TODAY IS:

MY CONFIDENCE LEVEL IS:

Low　1　　　2　　　3　　　4　　　5　High

MY INTERNAL PERFORMANCE STATE LEVEL IS:

1　2　3　4　5　6　7　8　9　10
Low Energy Level　　　　　　　　　　High Energy Level

IDENTIFY/DESCRIBE SIGNAL LIGHTS I RECOGNIZED: Green – Yellow – Red

HOW DID I RELEASE MY YELLOW/RED LIGHTS?

Circle One: TRAINING DAY or COMPETITION DAY

WHAT DID I DO WELL TODAY? What Gets Rewarded Gets Repeated.

WHAT CAN I DO BETTER? The Struggle Is Necessary In Order To Learn, Grow, and Evolve.

HOW CAN I DO IT DIFFERENTLY? Keep It Super Simple. Be The Best At Getting Better.

TODAY I LEARNED THAT:

MY PERFORMANCE EVALUATION:

1   2   3   4   5   6   8   9   10

Did you notice there is not a #7 on the performance evaluation? You are working to be elite and extraordinary, instead of average and mediocre. Your evaluation may include, but is not limited to: your mindset – your focus – being goal-driven and purposeful – progression of skills – effort given – energy level – emotional regulation – getting outside of your comfort zone – using obstacles as an opportunity to grow – learning from your experience – helping others to get better.

DATE: M   T   W   TH   F   S   S

GHP PRINCIPLE: 3 THINGS I AM GRATEFUL FOR TODAY.

1.
2.
3.

NOTABLE DETAILS OF MY TRAINING/COMPETITION.

MY GOAL TODAY IS:

MY CONFIDENCE LEVEL IS:

Low   1   2   3   4   5   High

MY INTERNAL PERFORMANCE STATE LEVEL IS:

1   2   3   4   5   6   7   8   9   10
Low Energy Level ←————————————————→ High Energy Level

IDENTIFY/DESCRIBE SIGNAL LIGHTS I RECOGNIZED: Green – Yellow – Red

HOW DID I RELEASE MY YELLOW/RED LIGHTS?

Circle One: TRAINING DAY or COMPETITION DAY

WHAT DID I DO WELL TODAY? What Gets Rewarded Gets Repeated.

WHAT CAN I DO BETTER? The Struggle Is Necessary In Order To Learn, Grow, and Evolve.

HOW CAN I DO IT DIFFERENTLY? Keep It Super Simple. Be The Best At Getting Better.

TODAY I LEARNED THAT:

MY PERFORMANCE EVALUATION:

1   2   3   4   5   6   8   9   10

Did you notice there is not a #7 on the performance evaluation? You are working to be elite and extraordinary, instead of average and mediocre. Your evaluation may include, but is not limited to: your mindset – your focus – being goal-driven and purposeful – progression of skills – effort given – energy level – emotional regulation – getting outside of your comfort zone – using obstacles as an opportunity to grow – learning from your experience – helping others to get better.

DATE: M T W TH F S S

GHP PRINCIPLE: 3 THINGS I AM GRATEFUL FOR TODAY.

1.

2.

3.

NOTABLE DETAILS OF MY TRAINING/COMPETITION.

MY GOAL TODAY IS:

MY CONFIDENCE LEVEL IS:

Low 1 2 3 4 5 High

MY INTERNAL PERFORMANCE STATE LEVEL IS:

1 2 3 4 5 6 7 8 9 10
Low Energy Level ←————————————→ High Energy Level

IDENTIFY/DESCRIBE SIGNAL LIGHTS I RECOGNIZED: Green – Yellow – Red

HOW DID I RELEASE MY YELLOW/RED LIGHTS?

Circle One: TRAINING DAY or COMPETITION DAY

WHAT DID I DO WELL TODAY? What Gets Rewarded Gets Repeated.

WHAT CAN I DO BETTER? The Struggle Is Necessary In Order To Learn, Grow, and Evolve.

HOW CAN I DO IT DIFFERENTLY? Keep It Super Simple. Be The Best At Getting Better.

TODAY I LEARNED THAT:

MY PERFORMANCE EVALUATION:

1   2   3   4   5   6   8   9   10

Did you notice there is not a #7 on the performance evaluation? You are working to be elite and extraordinary, instead of average and mediocre. Your evaluation may include, but is not limited to: your mindset – your focus – being goal-driven and purposeful – progression of skills – effort given – energy level – emotional regulation – getting outside of your comfort zone – using obstacles as an opportunity to grow – learning from your experience – helping others to get better.

DATE: M   T   W   TH   F   S   S

GHP PRINCIPLE: 3 THINGS I AM GRATEFUL FOR TODAY.

1.

2.

3.

NOTABLE DETAILS OF MY TRAINING/COMPETITION.

MY GOAL TODAY IS:

MY CONFIDENCE LEVEL IS:

Low 1   2   3   4   5 High

MY INTERNAL PERFORMANCE STATE LEVEL IS:

1   2   3   4   5   6   7   8   9   10
Low Energy Level ⟵⟶ High Energy Level

IDENTIFY/DESCRIBE SIGNAL LIGHTS I RECOGNIZED: Green – Yellow – Red

HOW DID I RELEASE MY YELLOW/RED LIGHTS?

Circle One: TRAINING DAY or COMPETITION DAY

WHAT DID I DO WELL TODAY? What Gets Rewarded Gets Repeated.

WHAT CAN I DO BETTER? The Struggle Is Necessary In Order To Learn, Grow, and Evolve.

HOW CAN I DO IT DIFFERENTLY? Keep It Super Simple. Be The Best At Getting Better.

TODAY I LEARNED THAT:

MY PERFORMANCE EVALUATION:

1   2   3   4   5   6   8   9   10

Did you notice there is not a #7 on the performance evaluation? You are working to be elite and extraordinary, instead of average and mediocre. Your evaluation may include, but is not limited to: your mindset – your focus – being goal-driven and purposeful – progression of skills – effort given – energy level – emotional regulation – getting outside of your comfort zone – using obstacles as an opportunity to grow – learning from your experience – helping others to get better.

DATE: M   T   W   TH   F   S   S

GHP PRINCIPLE: 3 THINGS I AM GRATEFUL FOR TODAY.

1.

2.

3.

NOTABLE DETAILS OF MY TRAINING/COMPETITION.

MY GOAL TODAY IS:

MY CONFIDENCE LEVEL IS:

       1   2   3   4   5

Low ⟵——————————————————⟶ High

MY INTERNAL PERFORMANCE STATE LEVEL IS:

1   2   3   4   5   6   7   8   9   10

Low Energy Level ⟵——————————⟶ High Energy Level

IDENTIFY/DESCRIBE SIGNAL LIGHTS I RECOGNIZED: Green – Yellow – Red

HOW DID I RELEASE MY YELLOW/RED LIGHTS?

Circle One: TRAINING DAY or COMPETITION DAY

WHAT DID I DO WELL TODAY? What Gets Rewarded Gets Repeated.

WHAT CAN I DO BETTER? The Struggle Is Necessary In Order To Learn, Grow, and Evolve.

HOW CAN I DO IT DIFFERENTLY? Keep It Super Simple. Be The Best At Getting Better.

TODAY I LEARNED THAT:

MY PERFORMANCE EVALUATION:

1   2   3   4   5   6   8   9   10

Did you notice there is not a #7 on the performance evaluation? You are working to be elite and extraordinary, instead of average and mediocre. Your evaluation may include, but is not limited to: your mindset – your focus – being goal-driven and purposeful – progression of skills – effort given – energy level – emotional regulation – getting outside of your comfort zone – using obstacles as an opportunity to grow – learning from your experience – helping others to get better.

DATE: M   T   W   TH   F   S   S

GHP PRINCIPLE: 3 THINGS I AM GRATEFUL FOR TODAY.

1.

2.

3.

NOTABLE DETAILS OF MY TRAINING/COMPETITION.

MY GOAL TODAY IS:

MY CONFIDENCE LEVEL IS:

Low   1   2   3   4   5   High

MY INTERNAL PERFORMANCE STATE LEVEL IS:

1   2   3   4   5   6   7   8   9   10

Low Energy Level   ⟵⟶   High Energy Level

IDENTIFY/DESCRIBE SIGNAL LIGHTS I RECOGNIZED: Green – Yellow – Red

HOW DID I RELEASE MY YELLOW/RED LIGHTS?

Circle One: TRAINING DAY or COMPETITION DAY

WHAT DID I DO WELL TODAY? What Gets Rewarded Gets Repeated.

WHAT CAN I DO BETTER? The Struggle Is Necessary In Order To Learn, Grow, and Evolve.

HOW CAN I DO IT DIFFERENTLY? Keep It Super Simple. Be The Best At Getting Better.

TODAY I LEARNED THAT:

MY PERFORMANCE EVALUATION:

1   2   3   4   5   6   8   9   10

Did you notice there is not a #7 on the performance evaluation? You are working to be elite and extraordinary, instead of average and mediocre. Your evaluation may include, but is not limited to: your mindset – your focus – being goal-driven and purposeful – progression of skills – effort given – energy level – emotional regulation – getting outside of your comfort zone – using obstacles as an opportunity to grow – learning from your experience – helping others to get better.

DATE: M   T   W   TH   F   S   S

GHP PRINCIPLE: 3 THINGS I AM GRATEFUL FOR TODAY.

1.

2.

3.

NOTABLE DETAILS OF MY TRAINING/COMPETITION.

MY GOAL TODAY IS:

MY CONFIDENCE LEVEL IS:

```
         1              2              3              4              5
Low ←                                                                   → High
```

MY INTERNAL PERFORMANCE STATE LEVEL IS:

```
 1    2    3    4    5    6    7    8    9    10
Low Energy Level ←                        → High Energy Level
```

IDENTIFY/DESCRIBE SIGNAL LIGHTS I RECOGNIZED: Green – Yellow – Red

HOW DID I RELEASE MY YELLOW/RED LIGHTS?

Circle One: TRAINING DAY or COMPETITION DAY

WHAT DID I DO WELL TODAY? What Gets Rewarded Gets Repeated.

WHAT CAN I DO BETTER? The Struggle Is Necessary In Order To Learn, Grow, and Evolve.

HOW CAN I DO IT DIFFERENTLY? Keep It Super Simple. Be The Best At Getting Better.

TODAY I LEARNED THAT:

MY PERFORMANCE EVALUATION:

1   2   3   4   5   6   8   9   10

Did you notice there is not a #7 on the performance evaluation? You are working to be elite and extraordinary, instead of average and mediocre. Your evaluation may include, but is not limited to: your mindset – your focus – being goal-driven and purposeful – progression of skills – effort given – energy level – emotional regulation – getting outside of your comfort zone – using obstacles as an opportunity to grow – learning from your experience – helping others to get better.

DATE: M   T   W   TH   F   S   S

GHP PRINCIPLE: 3 THINGS I AM GRATEFUL FOR TODAY.

1.

2.

3.

NOTABLE DETAILS OF MY TRAINING/COMPETITION.

MY GOAL TODAY IS:

MY CONFIDENCE LEVEL IS:

Low   1   2   3   4   5   High

MY INTERNAL PERFORMANCE STATE LEVEL IS:

1   2   3   4   5   6   7   8   9   10

Low Energy Level ⟵⟶ High Energy Level

IDENTIFY/DESCRIBE SIGNAL LIGHTS I RECOGNIZED: Green – Yellow – Red

HOW DID I RELEASE MY YELLOW/RED LIGHTS?

Circle One: TRAINING DAY or COMPETITION DAY

WHAT DID I DO WELL TODAY? What Gets Rewarded Gets Repeated.

WHAT CAN I DO BETTER? The Struggle Is Necessary In Order To Learn, Grow, and Evolve.

HOW CAN I DO IT DIFFERENTLY? Keep It Super Simple. Be The Best At Getting Better.

TODAY I LEARNED THAT:

MY PERFORMANCE EVALUATION:

1   2   3   4   5   6   8   9   10

Did you notice there is not a #7 on the performance evaluation? You are working to be elite and extraordinary, instead of average and mediocre. Your evaluation may include, but is not limited to: your mindset – your focus – being goal-driven and purposeful – progression of skills – effort given – energy level – emotional regulation – getting outside of your comfort zone – using obstacles as an opportunity to grow – learning from your experience – helping others to get better.

DATE: M   T   W   TH   F   S   S

GHP PRINCIPLE: 3 THINGS I AM GRATEFUL FOR TODAY.

1.
2.
3.

NOTABLE DETAILS OF MY TRAINING/COMPETITION.

MY GOAL TODAY IS:

MY CONFIDENCE LEVEL IS:

Low   1   2   3   4   5   High

MY INTERNAL PERFORMANCE STATE LEVEL IS:

1   2   3   4   5   6   7   8   9   10

Low Energy Level   High Energy Level

IDENTIFY/DESCRIBE SIGNAL LIGHTS I RECOGNIZED: Green – Yellow – Red

HOW DID I RELEASE MY YELLOW/RED LIGHTS?

Circle One: TRAINING DAY or COMPETITION DAY

WHAT DID I DO WELL TODAY? What Gets Rewarded Gets Repeated.

WHAT CAN I DO BETTER? The Struggle Is Necessary In Order To Learn, Grow, and Evolve.

HOW CAN I DO IT DIFFERENTLY? Keep It Super Simple. Be The Best At Getting Better.

TODAY I LEARNED THAT:

MY PERFORMANCE EVALUATION:

1   2   3   4   5   6   8   9   10

Did you notice there is not a #7 on the performance evaluation? You are working to be elite and extraordinary, instead of average and mediocre. Your evaluation may include, but is not limited to: your mindset – your focus – being goal-driven and purposeful – progression of skills – effort given – energy level – emotional regulation – getting outside of your comfort zone – using obstacles as an opportunity to grow – learning from your experience – helping others to get better.

DATE: M   T   W   TH   F   S   S

GHP PRINCIPLE: 3 THINGS I AM GRATEFUL FOR TODAY.

1.
2.
3.

NOTABLE DETAILS OF MY TRAINING/COMPETITION.

MY GOAL TODAY IS:

MY CONFIDENCE LEVEL IS:

Low   1   2   3   4   5   High

MY INTERNAL PERFORMANCE STATE LEVEL IS:

1   2   3   4   5   6   7   8   9   10

Low Energy Level ⟵⟶ High Energy Level

IDENTIFY/DESCRIBE SIGNAL LIGHTS I RECOGNIZED: Green – Yellow – Red

HOW DID I RELEASE MY YELLOW/RED LIGHTS?

Circle One: TRAINING DAY or COMPETITION DAY

WHAT DID I DO WELL TODAY? What Gets Rewarded Gets Repeated.

WHAT CAN I DO BETTER? The Struggle Is Necessary In Order To Learn, Grow, and Evolve.

HOW CAN I DO IT DIFFERENTLY? Keep It Super Simple. Be The Best At Getting Better.

TODAY I LEARNED THAT:

MY PERFORMANCE EVALUATION:

1   2   3   4   5   6   8   9   10

Did you notice there is not a #7 on the performance evaluation? You are working to be elite and extraordinary, instead of average and mediocre. Your evaluation may include, but is not limited to: your mindset – your focus – being goal-driven and purposeful – progression of skills – effort given – energy level – emotional regulation – getting outside of your comfort zone – using obstacles as an opportunity to grow – learning from your experience – helping others to get better.

DAILY PERFORMANCE JOURNAL PAGES

DATE: M T W TH F S S

GHP PRINCIPLE: 3 THINGS I AM GRATEFUL FOR TODAY.

1.

2.

3.

NOTABLE DETAILS OF MY TRAINING/COMPETITION.

MY GOAL TODAY IS:

MY CONFIDENCE LEVEL IS:

Low 1 2 3 4 5 High

MY INTERNAL PERFORMANCE STATE LEVEL IS:

1 2 3 4 5 6 7 8 9 10

Low Energy Level ⟵⟶ High Energy Level

IDENTIFY/DESCRIBE SIGNAL LIGHTS I RECOGNIZED: Green – Yellow – Red

HOW DID I RELEASE MY YELLOW/RED LIGHTS?

Circle One: TRAINING DAY or COMPETITION DAY

WHAT DID I DO WELL TODAY? What Gets Rewarded Gets Repeated.

WHAT CAN I DO BETTER? The Struggle Is Necessary In Order To Learn, Grow, and Evolve.

HOW CAN I DO IT DIFFERENTLY? Keep It Super Simple. Be The Best At Getting Better.

TODAY I LEARNED THAT:

MY PERFORMANCE EVALUATION:

1   2   3   4   5   6   8   9   10

Did you notice there is not a #7 on the performance evaluation? You are working to be elite and extraordinary, instead of average and mediocre. Your evaluation may include, but is not limited to: your mindset – your focus – being goal-driven and purposeful – progression of skills – effort given – energy level – emotional regulation – getting outside of your comfort zone – using obstacles as an opportunity to grow – learning from your experience – helping others to get better.

DATE: M   T   W   TH   F   S   S

GHP PRINCIPLE: 3 THINGS I AM GRATEFUL FOR TODAY.

1.

2.

3.

NOTABLE DETAILS OF MY TRAINING/COMPETITION.

MY GOAL TODAY IS:

MY CONFIDENCE LEVEL IS:

Low   1   2   3   4   5   High

MY INTERNAL PERFORMANCE STATE LEVEL IS:

1   2   3   4   5   6   7   8   9   10

Low Energy Level   High Energy Level

IDENTIFY/DESCRIBE SIGNAL LIGHTS I RECOGNIZED: Green – Yellow – Red

HOW DID I RELEASE MY YELLOW/RED LIGHTS?

Circle One: TRAINING DAY or COMPETITION DAY

WHAT DID I DO WELL TODAY? What Gets Rewarded Gets Repeated.

WHAT CAN I DO BETTER? The Struggle Is Necessary In Order To Learn, Grow, and Evolve.

HOW CAN I DO IT DIFFERENTLY? Keep It Super Simple. Be The Best At Getting Better.

TODAY I LEARNED THAT:

MY PERFORMANCE EVALUATION:

1   2   3   4   5   6   8   9   10

Did you notice there is not a #7 on the performance evaluation? You are working to be elite and extraordinary, instead of average and mediocre. Your evaluation may include, but is not limited to: your mindset – your focus – being goal-driven and purposeful – progression of skills – effort given – energy level – emotional regulation – getting outside of your comfort zone – using obstacles as an opportunity to grow – learning from your experience – helping others to get better.

DATE: M   T   W   TH   F   S   S

GHP PRINCIPLE: 3 THINGS I AM GRATEFUL FOR TODAY.

1.

2.

3.

NOTABLE DETAILS OF MY TRAINING/COMPETITION.

MY GOAL TODAY IS:

MY CONFIDENCE LEVEL IS:

Low   1   2   3   4   5   High

MY INTERNAL PERFORMANCE STATE LEVEL IS:

1   2   3   4   5   6   7   8   9   10

Low Energy Level ⟷ High Energy Level

IDENTIFY/DESCRIBE SIGNAL LIGHTS I RECOGNIZED: Green – Yellow – Red

HOW DID I RELEASE MY YELLOW/RED LIGHTS?

Circle One: TRAINING DAY or COMPETITION DAY

WHAT DID I DO WELL TODAY? What Gets Rewarded Gets Repeated.

WHAT CAN I DO BETTER? The Struggle Is Necessary In Order To Learn, Grow, and Evolve.

HOW CAN I DO IT DIFFERENTLY? Keep It Super Simple. Be The Best At Getting Better.

TODAY I LEARNED THAT:

MY PERFORMANCE EVALUATION:

1   2   3   4   5   6   8   9   10

Did you notice there is not a #7 on the performance evaluation? You are working to be elite and extraordinary, instead of average and mediocre. Your evaluation may include, but is not limited to: your mindset – your focus – being goal-driven and purposeful – progression of skills – effort given – energy level – emotional regulation – getting outside of your comfort zone – using obstacles as an opportunity to grow – learning from your experience – helping others to get better.

DATE: .... M T W TH F S S

GHP PRINCIPLE: 3 THINGS I AM GRATEFUL FOR TODAY.

1.

2.

3.

NOTABLE DETAILS OF MY TRAINING/COMPETITION.

MY GOAL TODAY IS:

MY CONFIDENCE LEVEL IS:

```
         1              2              3              4              5
Low ←                                                                    → High
```

MY INTERNAL PERFORMANCE STATE LEVEL IS:

```
1    2    3    4    5    6    7    8    9    10
Low Energy Level  ←                    →  High Energy Level
```

IDENTIFY/DESCRIBE SIGNAL LIGHTS I RECOGNIZED: Green – Yellow – Red

HOW DID I RELEASE MY YELLOW/RED LIGHTS?

Circle One: TRAINING DAY or COMPETITION DAY

WHAT DID I DO WELL TODAY? What Gets Rewarded Gets Repeated.

WHAT CAN I DO BETTER? The Struggle Is Necessary In Order To Learn, Grow, and Evolve.

HOW CAN I DO IT DIFFERENTLY? Keep It Super Simple. Be The Best At Getting Better.

TODAY I LEARNED THAT:

MY PERFORMANCE EVALUATION:

1   2   3   4   5   6   8   9   10

Did you notice there is not a #7 on the performance evaluation? You are working to be elite and extraordinary, instead of average and mediocre. Your evaluation may include, but is not limited to: your mindset – your focus – being goal-driven and purposeful – progression of skills – effort given – energy level – emotional regulation – getting outside of your comfort zone – using obstacles as an opportunity to grow – learning from your experience – helping others to get better.

DATE: M   T   W   TH   F   S   S

GHP PRINCIPLE: 3 THINGS I AM GRATEFUL FOR TODAY.

1.

2.

3.

NOTABLE DETAILS OF MY TRAINING/COMPETITION.

MY GOAL TODAY IS:

MY CONFIDENCE LEVEL IS:

1   2   3   4   5

Low ←————————————————————→ High

MY INTERNAL PERFORMANCE STATE LEVEL IS:

1   2   3   4   5   6   7   8   9   10

Low Energy Level ←————————————→ High Energy Level

IDENTIFY/DESCRIBE SIGNAL LIGHTS I RECOGNIZED: Green – Yellow – Red

HOW DID I RELEASE MY YELLOW/RED LIGHTS?

Circle One: TRAINING DAY or COMPETITION DAY

WHAT DID I DO <u>WELL</u> TODAY? What Gets Rewarded Gets Repeated.

WHAT CAN I DO <u>BETTER</u>? The Struggle Is Necessary In Order To Learn, Grow, and Evolve.

<u>HOW</u> CAN I DO IT DIFFERENTLY? Keep It Super Simple. Be The Best At Getting Better.

TODAY I LEARNED THAT:

MY PERFORMANCE EVALUATION:

1   2   3   4   5   6   8   9   10

Did you notice there is not a #7 on the performance evaluation? You are working to be elite and extraordinary, instead of average and mediocre. Your evaluation may include, but is not limited to: your mindset – your focus – being goal-driven and purposeful – progression of skills – effort given – energy level – emotional regulation – getting outside of your comfort zone – using obstacles as an opportunity to grow – learning from your experience – helping others to get better.

DATE: M   T   W   TH   F   S   S

GHP PRINCIPLE: 3 THINGS I AM GRATEFUL FOR TODAY.

1.

2.

3.

NOTABLE DETAILS OF MY TRAINING/COMPETITION.

MY GOAL TODAY IS:

MY CONFIDENCE LEVEL IS:

Low   1   2   3   4   5   High

MY INTERNAL PERFORMANCE STATE LEVEL IS:

1   2   3   4   5   6   7   8   9   10

Low Energy Level ⟵⟶ High Energy Level

IDENTIFY/DESCRIBE SIGNAL LIGHTS I RECOGNIZED: Green – Yellow – Red

HOW DID I RELEASE MY YELLOW/RED LIGHTS?

Circle One: TRAINING DAY or COMPETITION DAY

WHAT DID I DO <u>WELL</u> TODAY? What Gets Rewarded Gets Repeated.

WHAT CAN I DO <u>BETTER</u>? The Struggle Is Necessary In Order To Learn, Grow, and Evolve.

<u>HOW</u> CAN I DO IT DIFFERENTLY? Keep It Super Simple. Be The Best At Getting Better.

TODAY I LEARNED THAT:

MY PERFORMANCE EVALUATION:

1   2   3   4   5   6   8   9   10

Did you notice there is not a #7 on the performance evaluation? You are working to be elite and extraordinary, instead of average and mediocre. Your evaluation may include, but is not limited to: your mindset – your focus – being goal-driven and purposeful – progression of skills – effort given – energy level – emotional regulation – getting outside of your comfort zone – using obstacles as an opportunity to grow – learning from your experience – helping others to get better.

DATE: M   T   W   TH   F   S   S

GHP PRINCIPLE: 3 THINGS I AM GRATEFUL FOR TODAY.

1.
2.
3.

NOTABLE DETAILS OF MY TRAINING/COMPETITION.

MY GOAL TODAY IS:

MY CONFIDENCE LEVEL IS:

Low   1   2   3   4   5   High

MY INTERNAL PERFORMANCE STATE LEVEL IS:

1   2   3   4   5   6   7   8   9   10

Low Energy Level ⟵⟶ High Energy Level

IDENTIFY/DESCRIBE SIGNAL LIGHTS I RECOGNIZED: Green – Yellow – Red

HOW DID I RELEASE MY YELLOW/RED LIGHTS?

Circle One: TRAINING DAY or COMPETITION DAY

WHAT DID I DO WELL TODAY? What Gets Rewarded Gets Repeated.

WHAT CAN I DO BETTER? The Struggle Is Necessary In Order To Learn, Grow, and Evolve.

HOW CAN I DO IT DIFFERENTLY? Keep It Super Simple. Be The Best At Getting Better.

TODAY I LEARNED THAT:

MY PERFORMANCE EVALUATION:

1   2   3   4   5   6   8   9   10

Did you notice there is not a #7 on the performance evaluation? You are working to be elite and extraordinary, instead of average and mediocre. Your evaluation may include, but is not limited to: your mindset – your focus – being goal-driven and purposeful – progression of skills – effort given – energy level – emotional regulation – getting outside of your comfort zone – using obstacles as an opportunity to grow – learning from your experience – helping others to get better.

DATE: M   T   W   TH   F   S   S

GHP PRINCIPLE: 3 THINGS I AM GRATEFUL FOR TODAY.

1.

2.

3.

NOTABLE DETAILS OF MY TRAINING/COMPETITION.

MY GOAL TODAY IS:

MY CONFIDENCE LEVEL IS:

Low   1   2   3   4   5   High

MY INTERNAL PERFORMANCE STATE LEVEL IS:

1   2   3   4   5   6   7   8   9   10

Low Energy Level ⟷ High Energy Level

IDENTIFY/DESCRIBE SIGNAL LIGHTS I RECOGNIZED: Green – Yellow – Red

HOW DID I RELEASE MY YELLOW/RED LIGHTS?

Circle One: TRAINING DAY or COMPETITION DAY

WHAT DID I DO WELL TODAY? What Gets Rewarded Gets Repeated.

WHAT CAN I DO BETTER? The Struggle Is Necessary In Order To Learn, Grow, and Evolve.

HOW CAN I DO IT DIFFERENTLY? Keep It Super Simple. Be The Best At Getting Better.

TODAY I LEARNED THAT:

MY PERFORMANCE EVALUATION:

1 2 3 4 5 6 8 9 10

Did you notice there is not a #7 on the performance evaluation? You are working to be elite and extraordinary, instead of average and mediocre. Your evaluation may include, but is not limited to: your mindset – your focus – being goal-driven and purposeful – progression of skills – effort given – energy level – emotional regulation – getting outside of your comfort zone – using obstacles as an opportunity to grow – learning from your experience – helping others to get better.

DATE: M   T   W   TH   F   S   S

GHP PRINCIPLE: 3 THINGS I AM GRATEFUL FOR TODAY.

1.

2.

3.

NOTABLE DETAILS OF MY TRAINING/COMPETITION.

MY GOAL TODAY IS:

MY CONFIDENCE LEVEL IS:

Low   1   2   3   4   5   High

MY INTERNAL PERFORMANCE STATE LEVEL IS:

1   2   3   4   5   6   7   8   9   10

Low Energy Level   High Energy Level

IDENTIFY/DESCRIBE SIGNAL LIGHTS I RECOGNIZED: Green – Yellow – Red

HOW DID I RELEASE MY YELLOW/RED LIGHTS?

Circle One: TRAINING DAY or COMPETITION DAY

WHAT DID I DO WELL TODAY? What Gets Rewarded Gets Repeated.

WHAT CAN I DO BETTER? The Struggle Is Necessary In Order To Learn, Grow, and Evolve.

HOW CAN I DO IT DIFFERENTLY? Keep It Super Simple. Be The Best At Getting Better.

TODAY I LEARNED THAT:

MY PERFORMANCE EVALUATION:

1   2   3   4   5   6   8   9   10

Did you notice there is not a #7 on the performance evaluation? You are working to be elite and extraordinary, instead of average and mediocre. Your evaluation may include, but is not limited to: your mindset – your focus – being goal-driven and purposeful – progression of skills – effort given – energy level – emotional regulation – getting outside of your comfort zone – using obstacles as an opportunity to grow – learning from your experience – helping others to get better.

DATE:　　　　　　　　　　　　　　　　　M　T　W　TH　F　S　S

GHP PRINCIPLE: 3 THINGS I AM GRATEFUL FOR TODAY.

1.

2.

3.

NOTABLE DETAILS OF MY TRAINING/COMPETITION.

MY GOAL TODAY IS:

MY CONFIDENCE LEVEL IS:

Low　1　　　2　　　3　　　4　　　5　High

MY INTERNAL PERFORMANCE STATE LEVEL IS:

1　2　3　4　5　6　7　8　9　10
Low Energy Level ←————————————→ High Energy Level

IDENTIFY/DESCRIBE SIGNAL LIGHTS I RECOGNIZED: Green – Yellow – Red

HOW DID I RELEASE MY YELLOW/RED LIGHTS?

Circle One: TRAINING DAY or COMPETITION DAY

WHAT DID I DO WELL TODAY? What Gets Rewarded Gets Repeated.

WHAT CAN I DO BETTER? The Struggle Is Necessary In Order To Learn, Grow, and Evolve.

HOW CAN I DO IT DIFFERENTLY? Keep It Super Simple. Be The Best At Getting Better.

TODAY I LEARNED THAT:

MY PERFORMANCE EVALUATION:

1   2   3   4   5   6   8   9   10

Did you notice there is not a #7 on the performance evaluation? You are working to be elite and extraordinary, instead of average and mediocre. Your evaluation may include, but is not limited to: your mindset – your focus – being goal-driven and purposeful – progression of skills – effort given – energy level – emotional regulation – getting outside of your comfort zone – using obstacles as an opportunity to grow – learning from your experience – helping others to get better.

DATE: .... M   T   W   TH   F   S   S

GHP PRINCIPLE: 3 THINGS I AM GRATEFUL FOR TODAY.

1.

2.

3.

NOTABLE DETAILS OF MY TRAINING/COMPETITION.

MY GOAL TODAY IS:

MY CONFIDENCE LEVEL IS:

Low 1 — 2 — 3 — 4 — 5 High

MY INTERNAL PERFORMANCE STATE LEVEL IS:

1 2 3 4 5 6 7 8 9 10
Low Energy Level ⟵————————⟶ High Energy Level

IDENTIFY/DESCRIBE SIGNAL LIGHTS I RECOGNIZED: Green – Yellow – Red

HOW DID I RELEASE MY YELLOW/RED LIGHTS?

Circle One: TRAINING DAY or COMPETITION DAY

WHAT DID I DO WELL TODAY? What Gets Rewarded Gets Repeated.

WHAT CAN I DO BETTER? The Struggle Is Necessary In Order To Learn, Grow, and Evolve.

HOW CAN I DO IT DIFFERENTLY? Keep It Super Simple. Be The Best At Getting Better.

TODAY I LEARNED THAT:

MY PERFORMANCE EVALUATION:

1   2   3   4   5   6   8   9   10

Did you notice there is not a #7 on the performance evaluation? You are working to be elite and extraordinary, instead of average and mediocre. Your evaluation may include, but is not limited to: your mindset – your focus – being goal-driven and purposeful – progression of skills – effort given – energy level – emotional regulation – getting outside of your comfort zone – using obstacles as an opportunity to grow – learning from your experience – helping others to get better.

DATE: M   T   W   TH   F   S   S

GHP PRINCIPLE: 3 THINGS I AM GRATEFUL FOR TODAY.

1.

2.

3.

NOTABLE DETAILS OF MY TRAINING/COMPETITION.

MY GOAL TODAY IS:

MY CONFIDENCE LEVEL IS:

Low   1   2   3   4   5   High

MY INTERNAL PERFORMANCE STATE LEVEL IS:

1   2   3   4   5   6   7   8   9   10

Low Energy Level ⟵⟶ High Energy Level

IDENTIFY/DESCRIBE SIGNAL LIGHTS I RECOGNIZED: Green – Yellow – Red

HOW DID I RELEASE MY YELLOW/RED LIGHTS?

Circle One: TRAINING DAY or COMPETITION DAY

WHAT DID I DO WELL TODAY? What Gets Rewarded Gets Repeated.

WHAT CAN I DO BETTER? The Struggle Is Necessary In Order To Learn, Grow, and Evolve.

HOW CAN I DO IT DIFFERENTLY? Keep It Super Simple. Be The Best At Getting Better.

TODAY I LEARNED THAT:

MY PERFORMANCE EVALUATION:

1   2   3   4   5   6   8   9   10

Did you notice there is not a #7 on the performance evaluation? You are working to be elite and extraordinary, instead of average and mediocre. Your evaluation may include, but is not limited to: your mindset – your focus – being goal-driven and purposeful – progression of skills – effort given – energy level – emotional regulation – getting outside of your comfort zone – using obstacles as an opportunity to grow – learning from your experience – helping others to get better.

DATE: M   T   W   TH   F   S   S

GHP PRINCIPLE: 3 THINGS I AM GRATEFUL FOR TODAY.

1.

2.

3.

NOTABLE DETAILS OF MY TRAINING/COMPETITION.

MY GOAL TODAY IS:

MY CONFIDENCE LEVEL IS:

       1   2   3   4   5

Low ←————————————————————→ High

MY INTERNAL PERFORMANCE STATE LEVEL IS:

1   2   3   4   5   6   7   8   9   10

Low Energy Level ←————————————→ High Energy Level

IDENTIFY/DESCRIBE SIGNAL LIGHTS I RECOGNIZED: Green – Yellow – Red

HOW DID I RELEASE MY YELLOW/RED LIGHTS?

Circle One: TRAINING DAY or COMPETITION DAY

WHAT DID I DO WELL TODAY? What Gets Rewarded Gets Repeated.

WHAT CAN I DO BETTER? The Struggle Is Necessary In Order To Learn, Grow, and Evolve.

HOW CAN I DO IT DIFFERENTLY? Keep It Super Simple. Be The Best At Getting Better.

TODAY I LEARNED THAT:

MY PERFORMANCE EVALUATION:

1   2   3   4   5   6   8   9   10

Did you notice there is not a #7 on the performance evaluation? You are working to be elite and extraordinary, instead of average and mediocre. Your evaluation may include, but is not limited to: your mindset – your focus – being goal-driven and purposeful – progression of skills – effort given – energy level – emotional regulation – getting outside of your comfort zone – using obstacles as an opportunity to grow – learning from your experience – helping others to get better.

DATE: M   T   W   TH   F   S   S

GHP PRINCIPLE: 3 THINGS I AM GRATEFUL FOR TODAY.

1.

2.

3.

NOTABLE DETAILS OF MY TRAINING/COMPETITION.

MY GOAL TODAY IS:

MY CONFIDENCE LEVEL IS:

Low   1   2   3   4   5   High

MY INTERNAL PERFORMANCE STATE LEVEL IS:

1   2   3   4   5   6   7   8   9   10

Low Energy Level ⟵⟶ High Energy Level

IDENTIFY/DESCRIBE SIGNAL LIGHTS I RECOGNIZED: Green – Yellow – Red

HOW DID I RELEASE MY YELLOW/RED LIGHTS?

Circle One: TRAINING DAY or COMPETITION DAY

WHAT DID I DO WELL TODAY? What Gets Rewarded Gets Repeated.

WHAT CAN I DO BETTER? The Struggle Is Necessary In Order To Learn, Grow, and Evolve.

HOW CAN I DO IT DIFFERENTLY? Keep It Super Simple. Be The Best At Getting Better.

TODAY I LEARNED THAT:

MY PERFORMANCE EVALUATION:

1   2   3   4   5   6   8   9   10

Did you notice there is not a #7 on the performance evaluation? You are working to be elite and extraordinary, instead of average and mediocre. Your evaluation may include, but is not limited to: your mindset – your focus – being goal-driven and purposeful – progression of skills – effort given – energy level – emotional regulation – getting outside of your comfort zone – using obstacles as an opportunity to grow – learning from your experience – helping others to get better.

DATE: M   T   W   TH   F   S   S

GHP PRINCIPLE: 3 THINGS I AM GRATEFUL FOR TODAY.

1.

2.

3.

NOTABLE DETAILS OF MY TRAINING/COMPETITION.

MY GOAL TODAY IS:

MY CONFIDENCE LEVEL IS:

       1   2   3   4   5
Low ←   → High

MY INTERNAL PERFORMANCE STATE LEVEL IS:

1   2   3   4   5   6   7   8   9   10
Low Energy Level ←   → High Energy Level

IDENTIFY/DESCRIBE SIGNAL LIGHTS I RECOGNIZED: Green – Yellow – Red

HOW DID I RELEASE MY YELLOW/RED LIGHTS?

Circle One: TRAINING DAY or COMPETITION DAY

WHAT DID I DO WELL TODAY? What Gets Rewarded Gets Repeated.

WHAT CAN I DO BETTER? The Struggle Is Necessary In Order To Learn, Grow, and Evolve.

HOW CAN I DO IT DIFFERENTLY? Keep It Super Simple. Be The Best At Getting Better.

TODAY I LEARNED THAT:

MY PERFORMANCE EVALUATION:

1   2   3   4   5   6   8   9   10

Did you notice there is not a #7 on the performance evaluation? You are working to be elite and extraordinary, instead of average and mediocre. Your evaluation may include, but is not limited to: your mindset – your focus – being goal-driven and purposeful – progression of skills – effort given – energy level – emotional regulation – getting outside of your comfort zone – using obstacles as an opportunity to grow – learning from your experience – helping others to get better.

DATE: M   T   W   TH   F   S   S

GHP PRINCIPLE: 3 THINGS I AM GRATEFUL FOR TODAY.

1.

2.

3.

NOTABLE DETAILS OF MY TRAINING/COMPETITION.

MY GOAL TODAY IS:

MY CONFIDENCE LEVEL IS:

Low 1   2   3   4   5 High

MY INTERNAL PERFORMANCE STATE LEVEL IS:

1   2   3   4   5   6   7   8   9   10
Low Energy Level ←——————————————————→ High Energy Level

IDENTIFY/DESCRIBE SIGNAL LIGHTS I RECOGNIZED: Green – Yellow – Red

HOW DID I RELEASE MY YELLOW/RED LIGHTS?

Circle One: TRAINING DAY or COMPETITION DAY

WHAT DID I DO WELL TODAY? What Gets Rewarded Gets Repeated.

WHAT CAN I DO BETTER? The Struggle Is Necessary In Order To Learn, Grow, and Evolve.

HOW CAN I DO IT DIFFERENTLY? Keep It Super Simple. Be The Best At Getting Better.

TODAY I LEARNED THAT:

MY PERFORMANCE EVALUATION:

1   2   3   4   5   6   8   9   10

Did you notice there is not a #7 on the performance evaluation? You are working to be elite and extraordinary, instead of average and mediocre. Your evaluation may include, but is not limited to: your mindset – your focus – being goal-driven and purposeful – progression of skills – effort given – energy level – emotional regulation – getting outside of your comfort zone – using obstacles as an opportunity to grow – learning from your experience – helping others to get better.

DATE: M   T   W   TH   F   S   S

GHP PRINCIPLE: 3 THINGS I AM GRATEFUL FOR TODAY.

1.

2.

3.

NOTABLE DETAILS OF MY TRAINING/COMPETITION.

MY GOAL TODAY IS:

MY CONFIDENCE LEVEL IS:

Low   1   2   3   4   5   High

MY INTERNAL PERFORMANCE STATE LEVEL IS:

1   2   3   4   5   6   7   8   9   10

Low Energy Level ⟵————————————⟶ High Energy Level

IDENTIFY/DESCRIBE SIGNAL LIGHTS I RECOGNIZED: Green – Yellow – Red

HOW DID I RELEASE MY YELLOW/RED LIGHTS?

Circle One: TRAINING DAY or COMPETITION DAY

WHAT DID I DO WELL TODAY? What Gets Rewarded Gets Repeated.

WHAT CAN I DO BETTER? The Struggle Is Necessary In Order To Learn, Grow, and Evolve.

HOW CAN I DO IT DIFFERENTLY? Keep It Super Simple. Be The Best At Getting Better.

TODAY I LEARNED THAT:

MY PERFORMANCE EVALUATION:

1   2   3   4   5   6   8   9   10

Did you notice there is not a #7 on the performance evaluation? You are working to be elite and extraordinary, instead of average and mediocre. Your evaluation may include, but is not limited to: your mindset – your focus – being goal-driven and purposeful – progression of skills – effort given – energy level – emotional regulation – getting outside of your comfort zone – using obstacles as an opportunity to grow – learning from your experience – helping others to get better.

DATE: M   T   W   TH   F   S   S

GHP PRINCIPLE: 3 THINGS I AM GRATEFUL FOR TODAY.

1.
2.
3.

NOTABLE DETAILS OF MY TRAINING/COMPETITION.

MY GOAL TODAY IS:

MY CONFIDENCE LEVEL IS:

Low 1   2   3   4   5 High

MY INTERNAL PERFORMANCE STATE LEVEL IS:

1   2   3   4   5   6   7   8   9   10
Low Energy Level ←————————————————→ High Energy Level

IDENTIFY/DESCRIBE SIGNAL LIGHTS I RECOGNIZED: Green – Yellow – Red

HOW DID I RELEASE MY YELLOW/RED LIGHTS?

Circle One: TRAINING DAY or COMPETITION DAY

WHAT DID I DO WELL TODAY? What Gets Rewarded Gets Repeated.

WHAT CAN I DO BETTER? The Struggle Is Necessary In Order To Learn, Grow, and Evolve.

HOW CAN I DO IT DIFFERENTLY? Keep It Super Simple. Be The Best At Getting Better.

TODAY I LEARNED THAT:

MY PERFORMANCE EVALUATION:

1   2   3   4   5   6   8   9   10

Did you notice there is not a #7 on the performance evaluation? You are working to be elite and extraordinary, instead of average and mediocre. Your evaluation may include, but is not limited to: your mindset – your focus – being goal-driven and purposeful – progression of skills – effort given – energy level – emotional regulation – getting outside of your comfort zone – using obstacles as an opportunity to grow – learning from your experience – helping others to get better.

DATE: M   T   W   TH   F   S   S

GHP PRINCIPLE: 3 THINGS I AM GRATEFUL FOR TODAY.

1.
2.
3.

NOTABLE DETAILS OF MY TRAINING/COMPETITION.

MY GOAL TODAY IS:

MY CONFIDENCE LEVEL IS:

Low   1   2   3   4   5   High

MY INTERNAL PERFORMANCE STATE LEVEL IS:

1   2   3   4   5   6   7   8   9   10

Low Energy Level ⟵⟶ High Energy Level

IDENTIFY/DESCRIBE SIGNAL LIGHTS I RECOGNIZED: Green – Yellow – Red

HOW DID I RELEASE MY YELLOW/RED LIGHTS?

Circle One: TRAINING DAY or COMPETITION DAY

WHAT DID I DO WELL TODAY? What Gets Rewarded Gets Repeated.

WHAT CAN I DO BETTER? The Struggle Is Necessary In Order To Learn, Grow, and Evolve.

HOW CAN I DO IT DIFFERENTLY? Keep It Super Simple. Be The Best At Getting Better.

TODAY I LEARNED THAT:

MY PERFORMANCE EVALUATION:

1   2   3   4   5   6   8   9   10

Did you notice there is not a #7 on the performance evaluation? You are working to be elite and extraordinary, instead of average and mediocre. Your evaluation may include, but is not limited to: your mindset – your focus – being goal-driven and purposeful – progression of skills – effort given – energy level – emotional regulation – getting outside of your comfort zone – using obstacles as an opportunity to grow – learning from your experience – helping others to get better.

DATE:　　　　　　　　　　　　M　T　W　TH　F　S　S

GHP PRINCIPLE: 3 THINGS I AM GRATEFUL FOR TODAY.

1.

2.

3.

NOTABLE DETAILS OF MY TRAINING/COMPETITION.

MY GOAL TODAY IS:

MY CONFIDENCE LEVEL IS:

Low　1　　2　　3　　4　　5　High

MY INTERNAL PERFORMANCE STATE LEVEL IS:

1　2　3　4　5　6　7　8　9　10

Low Energy Level ←——————————————→ High Energy Level

IDENTIFY/DESCRIBE SIGNAL LIGHTS I RECOGNIZED: Green – Yellow – Red

HOW DID I RELEASE MY YELLOW/RED LIGHTS?

Circle One: TRAINING DAY or COMPETITION DAY

WHAT DID I DO WELL TODAY? What Gets Rewarded Gets Repeated.

WHAT CAN I DO BETTER? The Struggle Is Necessary In Order To Learn, Grow, and Evolve.

HOW CAN I DO IT DIFFERENTLY? Keep It Super Simple. Be The Best At Getting Better.

TODAY I LEARNED THAT:

MY PERFORMANCE EVALUATION:

1   2   3   4   5   6   8   9   10

Did you notice there is not a #7 on the performance evaluation? You are working to be elite and extraordinary, instead of average and mediocre. Your evaluation may include, but is not limited to: your mindset – your focus – being goal-driven and purposeful – progression of skills – effort given – energy level – emotional regulation – getting outside of your comfort zone – using obstacles as an opportunity to grow – learning from your experience – helping others to get better.

DATE: M   T   W   TH   F   S   S

GHP PRINCIPLE: 3 THINGS I AM GRATEFUL FOR TODAY.

1.
2.
3.

NOTABLE DETAILS OF MY TRAINING/COMPETITION.

MY GOAL TODAY IS:

MY CONFIDENCE LEVEL IS:

          1   2   3   4   5
Low ←   → High

MY INTERNAL PERFORMANCE STATE LEVEL IS:

1   2   3   4   5   6   7   8   9   10
Low Energy Level ←   → High Energy Level

IDENTIFY/DESCRIBE SIGNAL LIGHTS I RECOGNIZED: Green – Yellow – Red

HOW DID I RELEASE MY YELLOW/RED LIGHTS?

Circle One: TRAINING DAY or COMPETITION DAY

WHAT DID I DO WELL TODAY? What Gets Rewarded Gets Repeated.

WHAT CAN I DO BETTER? The Struggle Is Necessary In Order To Learn, Grow, and Evolve.

HOW CAN I DO IT DIFFERENTLY? Keep It Super Simple. Be The Best At Getting Better.

TODAY I LEARNED THAT:

MY PERFORMANCE EVALUATION:

1   2   3   4   5   6   8   9   10

Did you notice there is not a #7 on the performance evaluation? You are working to be elite and extraordinary, instead of average and mediocre. Your evaluation may include, but is not limited to: your mindset – your focus – being goal-driven and purposeful – progression of skills – effort given – energy level – emotional regulation – getting outside of your comfort zone – using obstacles as an opportunity to grow – learning from your experience – helping others to get better.

DATE: M   T   W   TH   F   S   S

GHP PRINCIPLE: 3 THINGS I AM GRATEFUL FOR TODAY.

1.
2.
3.

NOTABLE DETAILS OF MY TRAINING/COMPETITION.

MY GOAL TODAY IS:

MY CONFIDENCE LEVEL IS:

Low   1   2   3   4   5   High

MY INTERNAL PERFORMANCE STATE LEVEL IS:

1   2   3   4   5   6   7   8   9   10

Low Energy Level ⟵⟶ High Energy Level

IDENTIFY/DESCRIBE SIGNAL LIGHTS I RECOGNIZED: Green – Yellow – Red

HOW DID I RELEASE MY YELLOW/RED LIGHTS?

Circle One: TRAINING DAY or COMPETITION DAY

WHAT DID I DO WELL TODAY? What Gets Rewarded Gets Repeated.

WHAT CAN I DO BETTER? The Struggle Is Necessary In Order To Learn, Grow, and Evolve.

HOW CAN I DO IT DIFFERENTLY? Keep It Super Simple. Be The Best At Getting Better.

TODAY I LEARNED THAT:

MY PERFORMANCE EVALUATION:

1   2   3   4   5   6   8   9   10

Did you notice there is not a #7 on the performance evaluation? You are working to be elite and extraordinary, instead of average and mediocre. Your evaluation may include, but is not limited to: your mindset – your focus – being goal-driven and purposeful – progression of skills – effort given – energy level – emotional regulation – getting outside of your comfort zone – using obstacles as an opportunity to grow – learning from your experience – helping others to get better.

DATE: M   T   W   TH   F   S   S

GHP PRINCIPLE: 3 THINGS I AM GRATEFUL FOR TODAY.

1.

2.

3.

NOTABLE DETAILS OF MY TRAINING/COMPETITION.

MY GOAL TODAY IS:

MY CONFIDENCE LEVEL IS:

```
         1            2            3            4            5
Low ←                                                            → High
```

MY INTERNAL PERFORMANCE STATE LEVEL IS:

```
1    2    3    4    5    6    7    8    9    10
Low Energy Level ←                    → High Energy Level
```

IDENTIFY/DESCRIBE SIGNAL LIGHTS I RECOGNIZED: Green – Yellow – Red

HOW DID I RELEASE MY YELLOW/RED LIGHTS?

Circle One: TRAINING DAY or COMPETITION DAY

WHAT DID I DO WELL TODAY? What Gets Rewarded Gets Repeated.

WHAT CAN I DO BETTER? The Struggle Is Necessary In Order To Learn, Grow, and Evolve.

HOW CAN I DO IT DIFFERENTLY? Keep It Super Simple. Be The Best At Getting Better.

TODAY I LEARNED THAT:

MY PERFORMANCE EVALUATION:

1   2   3   4   5   6   8   9   10

Did you notice there is not a #7 on the performance evaluation? You are working to be elite and extraordinary, instead of average and mediocre. Your evaluation may include, but is not limited to: your mindset – your focus – being goal-driven and purposeful – progression of skills – effort given – energy level – emotional regulation – getting outside of your comfort zone – using obstacles as an opportunity to grow – learning from your experience – helping others to get better.

DATE: **M   T   W   TH   F   S   S**

GHP PRINCIPLE: 3 THINGS I AM GRATEFUL FOR TODAY.

1.

2.

3.

NOTABLE DETAILS OF MY TRAINING/COMPETITION.

MY GOAL TODAY IS:

MY CONFIDENCE LEVEL IS:

Low   1   2   3   4   5   High

MY INTERNAL PERFORMANCE STATE LEVEL IS:

1   2   3   4   5   6   7   8   9   10

Low Energy Level ⟵⟶ High Energy Level

IDENTIFY/DESCRIBE SIGNAL LIGHTS I RECOGNIZED: Green – Yellow – Red

HOW DID I RELEASE MY YELLOW/RED LIGHTS?

Circle One: TRAINING DAY or COMPETITION DAY

WHAT DID I DO WELL TODAY? What Gets Rewarded Gets Repeated.

WHAT CAN I DO BETTER? The Struggle Is Necessary In Order To Learn, Grow, and Evolve.

HOW CAN I DO IT DIFFERENTLY? Keep It Super Simple. Be The Best At Getting Better.

TODAY I LEARNED THAT:

MY PERFORMANCE EVALUATION:

1   2   3   4   5   6   8   9   10

Did you notice there is not a #7 on the performance evaluation? You are working to be elite and extraordinary, instead of average and mediocre. Your evaluation may include, but is not limited to: your mindset – your focus – being goal-driven and purposeful – progression of skills – effort given – energy level – emotional regulation – getting outside of your comfort zone – using obstacles as an opportunity to grow – learning from your experience – helping others to get better.

DATE: M   T   W   TH   F   S   S

GHP PRINCIPLE: 3 THINGS I AM GRATEFUL FOR TODAY.

1.

2.

3.

NOTABLE DETAILS OF MY TRAINING/COMPETITION.

MY GOAL TODAY IS:

MY CONFIDENCE LEVEL IS:

```
         1              2              3              4              5
Low  ←─────────────────────────────────────────────────────────→  High
```

MY INTERNAL PERFORMANCE STATE LEVEL IS:

```
1    2    3    4    5    6    7    8    9    10
Low Energy Level  ←──────────────────→  High Energy Level
```

IDENTIFY/DESCRIBE SIGNAL LIGHTS I RECOGNIZED: Green – Yellow – Red

HOW DID I RELEASE MY YELLOW/RED LIGHTS?

Circle One: TRAINING DAY or COMPETITION DAY

WHAT DID I DO WELL TODAY? What Gets Rewarded Gets Repeated.

WHAT CAN I DO BETTER? The Struggle Is Necessary In Order To Learn, Grow, and Evolve.

HOW CAN I DO IT DIFFERENTLY? Keep It Super Simple. Be The Best At Getting Better.

TODAY I LEARNED THAT:

MY PERFORMANCE EVALUATION:

1   2   3   4   5   6   8   9   10

Did you notice there is not a #7 on the performance evaluation? You are working to be elite and extraordinary, instead of average and mediocre. Your evaluation may include, but is not limited to: your mindset – your focus – being goal-driven and purposeful – progression of skills – effort given – energy level – emotional regulation – getting outside of your comfort zone – using obstacles as an opportunity to grow – learning from your experience – helping others to get better.

DATE: M   T   W   TH   F   S   S

GHP PRINCIPLE: 3 THINGS I AM GRATEFUL FOR TODAY.

1.
2.
3.

NOTABLE DETAILS OF MY TRAINING/COMPETITION.

MY GOAL TODAY IS:

MY CONFIDENCE LEVEL IS:

Low   1   2   3   4   5   High

MY INTERNAL PERFORMANCE STATE LEVEL IS:

1   2   3   4   5   6   7   8   9   10

Low Energy Level ⟵⟶ High Energy Level

IDENTIFY/DESCRIBE SIGNAL LIGHTS I RECOGNIZED: Green – Yellow – Red

HOW DID I RELEASE MY YELLOW/RED LIGHTS?

Circle One: TRAINING DAY or COMPETITION DAY

WHAT DID I DO <u>WELL</u> TODAY? What Gets Rewarded Gets Repeated.

WHAT CAN I DO <u>BETTER</u>? The Struggle Is Necessary In Order To Learn, Grow, and Evolve.

<u>HOW</u> CAN I DO IT DIFFERENTLY? Keep It Super Simple. Be The Best At Getting Better.

TODAY I LEARNED THAT:

MY PERFORMANCE EVALUATION:

1   2   3   4   5   6   8   9   10

Did you notice there is not a #7 on the performance evaluation? You are working to be elite and extraordinary, instead of average and mediocre. Your evaluation may include, but is not limited to: your mindset – your focus – being goal-driven and purposeful – progression of skills – effort given – energy level – emotional regulation – getting outside of your comfort zone – using obstacles as an opportunity to grow – learning from your experience – helping others to get better.

DATE: M   T   W   TH   F   S   S

GHP PRINCIPLE: 3 THINGS I AM GRATEFUL FOR TODAY.

1.

2.

3.

NOTABLE DETAILS OF MY TRAINING/COMPETITION.

MY GOAL TODAY IS:

MY CONFIDENCE LEVEL IS:

```
        1              2              3              4              5
Low  ←─────────────────────────────────────────────────────────────→  High
```

MY INTERNAL PERFORMANCE STATE LEVEL IS:

```
1     2     3     4     5     6     7     8     9     10
Low Energy Level ←──────────────────────→ High Energy Level
```

IDENTIFY/DESCRIBE SIGNAL LIGHTS I RECOGNIZED: Green – Yellow – Red

HOW DID I RELEASE MY YELLOW/RED LIGHTS?

Circle One: TRAINING DAY or COMPETITION DAY

WHAT DID I DO WELL TODAY? What Gets Rewarded Gets Repeated.

WHAT CAN I DO BETTER? The Struggle Is Necessary In Order To Learn, Grow, and Evolve.

HOW CAN I DO IT DIFFERENTLY? Keep It Super Simple. Be The Best At Getting Better.

TODAY I LEARNED THAT:

MY PERFORMANCE EVALUATION:

1   2   3   4   5   6   8   9   10

Did you notice there is not a #7 on the performance evaluation? You are working to be elite and extraordinary, instead of average and mediocre. Your evaluation may include, but is not limited to: your mindset – your focus – being goal-driven and purposeful – progression of skills – effort given – energy level – emotional regulation – getting outside of your comfort zone – using obstacles as an opportunity to grow – learning from your experience – helping others to get better.

DATE: M   T   W   TH   F   S   S

GHP PRINCIPLE: 3 THINGS I AM GRATEFUL FOR TODAY.

1.
2.
3.

NOTABLE DETAILS OF MY TRAINING/COMPETITION.

MY GOAL TODAY IS:

MY CONFIDENCE LEVEL IS:

Low   1   2   3   4   5   High

MY INTERNAL PERFORMANCE STATE LEVEL IS:

1   2   3   4   5   6   7   8   9   10

Low Energy Level ⟵⟶ High Energy Level

IDENTIFY/DESCRIBE SIGNAL LIGHTS I RECOGNIZED: Green – Yellow – Red

HOW DID I RELEASE MY YELLOW/RED LIGHTS?

Circle One: TRAINING DAY or COMPETITION DAY

WHAT DID I DO WELL TODAY? What Gets Rewarded Gets Repeated.

WHAT CAN I DO BETTER? The Struggle Is Necessary In Order To Learn, Grow, and Evolve.

HOW CAN I DO IT DIFFERENTLY? Keep It Super Simple. Be The Best At Getting Better.

TODAY I LEARNED THAT:

MY PERFORMANCE EVALUATION:

1   2   3   4   5   6   8   9   10

Did you notice there is not a #7 on the performance evaluation? You are working to be elite and extraordinary, instead of average and mediocre. Your evaluation may include, but is not limited to: your mindset – your focus – being goal-driven and purposeful – progression of skills – effort given – energy level – emotional regulation – getting outside of your comfort zone – using obstacles as an opportunity to grow – learning from your experience – helping others to get better.

DAILY PERFORMANCE JOURNAL PAGES • **183**

CONGRATULATIONS
IN CONSISTENTLY JOURNALING YOUR JOURNEY AND OPTIMIZING YOUR MENTAL PERFORMANCE!

Reminder

YOU HAVE 2 WEEKS LEFT BEFORE THIS PLAYBOOK IS COMPLETED.

I WANT TO ENCOURAGE YOU TO STAY COMMITTED TO BECOMING THE BEST AT GETTING BETTER.

REORDER YOUR NEW

MASTER THE ART OF WINNING
A Championship Playbook To Optimize Mental Performance

FROM AMAZON.

DATE: M   T   W   TH   F   S   S

GHP PRINCIPLE: 3 THINGS I AM GRATEFUL FOR TODAY.

1.

2.

3.

NOTABLE DETAILS OF MY TRAINING/COMPETITION.

MY GOAL TODAY IS:

MY CONFIDENCE LEVEL IS:

Low   1   2   3   4   5   High

MY INTERNAL PERFORMANCE STATE LEVEL IS:

1   2   3   4   5   6   7   8   9   10

Low Energy Level ⟷ High Energy Level

IDENTIFY/DESCRIBE SIGNAL LIGHTS I RECOGNIZED: Green – Yellow – Red

HOW DID I RELEASE MY YELLOW/RED LIGHTS?

Circle One: TRAINING DAY or COMPETITION DAY

WHAT DID I DO <u>WELL</u> TODAY? What Gets Rewarded Gets Repeated.

WHAT CAN I DO <u>BETTER</u>? The Struggle Is Necessary In Order To Learn, Grow, and Evolve.

<u>HOW</u> CAN I DO IT DIFFERENTLY? Keep It Super Simple. Be The Best At Getting Better.

TODAY I LEARNED THAT:

MY PERFORMANCE EVALUATION:

1   2   3   4   5   6   8   9   10

Did you notice there is not a #7 on the performance evaluation? You are working to be elite and extraordinary, instead of average and mediocre. Your evaluation may include, but is not limited to: your mindset – your focus – being goal-driven and purposeful – progression of skills – effort given – energy level – emotional regulation – getting outside of your comfort zone – using obstacles as an opportunity to grow – learning from your experience – helping others to get better.

DATE: M T W TH F S S

GHP PRINCIPLE: 3 THINGS I AM GRATEFUL FOR TODAY.

1.
2.
3.

NOTABLE DETAILS OF MY TRAINING/COMPETITION.

MY GOAL TODAY IS:

MY CONFIDENCE LEVEL IS:

Low ← 1   2   3   4   5 → High

MY INTERNAL PERFORMANCE STATE LEVEL IS:

1 2 3 4 5 6 7 8 9 10
Low Energy Level ← → High Energy Level

IDENTIFY/DESCRIBE SIGNAL LIGHTS I RECOGNIZED: Green – Yellow – Red

HOW DID I RELEASE MY YELLOW/RED LIGHTS?

Circle One: TRAINING DAY or COMPETITION DAY

WHAT DID I DO WELL TODAY? What Gets Rewarded Gets Repeated.

WHAT CAN I DO BETTER? The Struggle Is Necessary In Order To Learn, Grow, and Evolve.

HOW CAN I DO IT DIFFERENTLY? Keep It Super Simple. Be The Best At Getting Better.

TODAY I LEARNED THAT:

MY PERFORMANCE EVALUATION:

1   2   3   4   5   6   8   9   10

Did you notice there is not a #7 on the performance evaluation? You are working to be elite and extraordinary, instead of average and mediocre. Your evaluation may include, but is not limited to: your mindset – your focus – being goal-driven and purposeful – progression of skills – effort given – energy level – emotional regulation – getting outside of your comfort zone – using obstacles as an opportunity to grow – learning from your experience – helping others to get better.

DATE: M   T   W   TH   F   S   S

GHP PRINCIPLE: 3 THINGS I AM GRATEFUL FOR TODAY.

1.

2.

3.

NOTABLE DETAILS OF MY TRAINING/COMPETITION.

MY GOAL TODAY IS:

MY CONFIDENCE LEVEL IS:

Low   1   2   3   4   5   High

MY INTERNAL PERFORMANCE STATE LEVEL IS:

1   2   3   4   5   6   7   8   9   10

Low Energy Level   ⟵⟶   High Energy Level

IDENTIFY/DESCRIBE SIGNAL LIGHTS I RECOGNIZED: Green – Yellow – Red

HOW DID I RELEASE MY YELLOW/RED LIGHTS?

Circle One: TRAINING DAY or COMPETITION DAY

WHAT DID I DO WELL TODAY? What Gets Rewarded Gets Repeated.

WHAT CAN I DO BETTER? The Struggle Is Necessary In Order To Learn, Grow, and Evolve.

HOW CAN I DO IT DIFFERENTLY? Keep It Super Simple. Be The Best At Getting Better.

TODAY I LEARNED THAT:

MY PERFORMANCE EVALUATION:

1   2   3   4   5   6   8   9   10

Did you notice there is not a #7 on the performance evaluation? You are working to be elite and extraordinary, instead of average and mediocre. Your evaluation may include, but is not limited to: your mindset – your focus – being goal-driven and purposeful – progression of skills – effort given – energy level – emotional regulation – getting outside of your comfort zone – using obstacles as an opportunity to grow – learning from your experience – helping others to get better.

DATE: .... M   T   W   TH   F   S   S

GHP PRINCIPLE: 3 THINGS I AM GRATEFUL FOR TODAY.

1.

2.

3.

NOTABLE DETAILS OF MY TRAINING/COMPETITION.

MY GOAL TODAY IS:

MY CONFIDENCE LEVEL IS:

| 1 | 2 | 3 | 4 | 5 |

Low ←——————————————————————→ High

MY INTERNAL PERFORMANCE STATE LEVEL IS:

1   2   3   4   5   6   7   8   9   10

Low Energy Level ←——————————————————→ High Energy Level

IDENTIFY/DESCRIBE SIGNAL LIGHTS I RECOGNIZED: Green – Yellow – Red

HOW DID I RELEASE MY YELLOW/RED LIGHTS?

Circle One: TRAINING DAY or COMPETITION DAY

WHAT DID I DO WELL TODAY? What Gets Rewarded Gets Repeated.

WHAT CAN I DO BETTER? The Struggle Is Necessary In Order To Learn, Grow, and Evolve.

HOW CAN I DO IT DIFFERENTLY? Keep It Super Simple. Be The Best At Getting Better.

TODAY I LEARNED THAT:

MY PERFORMANCE EVALUATION:

1   2   3   4   5   6   8   9   10

Did you notice there is not a #7 on the performance evaluation? You are working to be elite and extraordinary, instead of average and mediocre. Your evaluation may include, but is not limited to: your mindset – your focus – being goal-driven and purposeful – progression of skills – effort given – energy level – emotional regulation – getting outside of your comfort zone – using obstacles as an opportunity to grow – learning from your experience – helping others to get better.

DAILY PERFORMANCE JOURNAL PAGES • 193

DATE: M   T   W   TH   F   S   S

GHP PRINCIPLE: 3 THINGS I AM GRATEFUL FOR TODAY.

1.
2.
3.

NOTABLE DETAILS OF MY TRAINING/COMPETITION.

MY GOAL TODAY IS:

MY CONFIDENCE LEVEL IS:

Low   1   2   3   4   5   High

MY INTERNAL PERFORMANCE STATE LEVEL IS:

1   2   3   4   5   6   7   8   9   10

Low Energy Level ⟵⟶ High Energy Level

IDENTIFY/DESCRIBE SIGNAL LIGHTS I RECOGNIZED: Green – Yellow – Red

HOW DID I RELEASE MY YELLOW/RED LIGHTS?

Circle One: TRAINING DAY or COMPETITION DAY

WHAT DID I DO WELL TODAY? What Gets Rewarded Gets Repeated.

WHAT CAN I DO BETTER? The Struggle Is Necessary In Order To Learn, Grow, and Evolve.

HOW CAN I DO IT DIFFERENTLY? Keep It Super Simple. Be The Best At Getting Better.

TODAY I LEARNED THAT:

MY PERFORMANCE EVALUATION:

1 2 3 4 5 6 8 9 10

Did you notice there is not a #7 on the performance evaluation? You are working to be elite and extraordinary, instead of average and mediocre. Your evaluation may include, but is not limited to: your mindset – your focus – being goal-driven and purposeful – progression of skills – effort given – energy level – emotional regulation – getting outside of your comfort zone – using obstacles as an opportunity to grow – learning from your experience – helping others to get better.

DATE: .... M T W TH F S S

GHP PRINCIPLE: 3 THINGS I AM GRATEFUL FOR TODAY.

1.
2.
3.

NOTABLE DETAILS OF MY TRAINING/COMPETITION.

MY GOAL TODAY IS:

MY CONFIDENCE LEVEL IS:

Low 1 2 3 4 5 High

MY INTERNAL PERFORMANCE STATE LEVEL IS:

1 2 3 4 5 6 7 8 9 10
Low Energy Level ←——————————————→ High Energy Level

IDENTIFY/DESCRIBE SIGNAL LIGHTS I RECOGNIZED: Green – Yellow – Red

HOW DID I RELEASE MY YELLOW/RED LIGHTS?

Circle One: TRAINING DAY or COMPETITION DAY

WHAT DID I DO WELL TODAY? What Gets Rewarded Gets Repeated.

WHAT CAN I DO BETTER? The Struggle Is Necessary In Order To Learn, Grow, and Evolve.

HOW CAN I DO IT DIFFERENTLY? Keep It Super Simple. Be The Best At Getting Better.

TODAY I LEARNED THAT:

MY PERFORMANCE EVALUATION:

1   2   3   4   5   6   8   9   10

Did you notice there is not a #7 on the performance evaluation? You are working to be elite and extraordinary, instead of average and mediocre. Your evaluation may include, but is not limited to: your mindset – your focus – being goal-driven and purposeful – progression of skills – effort given – energy level – emotional regulation – getting outside of your comfort zone – using obstacles as an opportunity to grow – learning from your experience – helping others to get better.

DATE: M   T   W   TH   F   S   S

GHP PRINCIPLE: 3 THINGS I AM GRATEFUL FOR TODAY.

1.
2.
3.

NOTABLE DETAILS OF MY TRAINING/COMPETITION.

MY GOAL TODAY IS:

MY CONFIDENCE LEVEL IS:

Low   1   2   3   4   5   High

MY INTERNAL PERFORMANCE STATE LEVEL IS:

1   2   3   4   5   6   7   8   9   10

Low Energy Level ⟵⟶ High Energy Level

IDENTIFY/DESCRIBE SIGNAL LIGHTS I RECOGNIZED: Green – Yellow – Red

HOW DID I RELEASE MY YELLOW/RED LIGHTS?

Circle One: TRAINING DAY or COMPETITION DAY

WHAT DID I DO WELL TODAY? What Gets Rewarded Gets Repeated.

WHAT CAN I DO BETTER? The Struggle Is Necessary In Order To Learn, Grow, and Evolve.

HOW CAN I DO IT DIFFERENTLY? Keep It Super Simple. Be The Best At Getting Better.

TODAY I LEARNED THAT:

MY PERFORMANCE EVALUATION:

1   2   3   4   5   6   8   9   10

Did you notice there is not a #7 on the performance evaluation? You are working to be elite and extraordinary, instead of average and mediocre. Your evaluation may include, but is not limited to: your mindset – your focus – being goal-driven and purposeful – progression of skills – effort given – energy level – emotional regulation – getting outside of your comfort zone – using obstacles as an opportunity to grow – learning from your experience – helping others to get better.

DATE: M   T   W   TH   F   S   S

GHP PRINCIPLE: 3 THINGS I AM GRATEFUL FOR TODAY.

1.
2.
3.

NOTABLE DETAILS OF MY TRAINING/COMPETITION.

MY GOAL TODAY IS:

MY CONFIDENCE LEVEL IS:

      1   2   3   4   5

Low ⟵——————————————⟶ High

MY INTERNAL PERFORMANCE STATE LEVEL IS:

1   2   3   4   5   6   7   8   9   10

Low Energy Level ⟵——————————⟶ High Energy Level

IDENTIFY/DESCRIBE SIGNAL LIGHTS I RECOGNIZED: Green – Yellow – Red

HOW DID I RELEASE MY YELLOW/RED LIGHTS?

Circle One: TRAINING DAY or COMPETITION DAY

WHAT DID I DO WELL TODAY? What Gets Rewarded Gets Repeated.

WHAT CAN I DO BETTER? The Struggle Is Necessary In Order To Learn, Grow, and Evolve.

HOW CAN I DO IT DIFFERENTLY? Keep It Super Simple. Be The Best At Getting Better.

TODAY I LEARNED THAT:

MY PERFORMANCE EVALUATION:

1   2   3   4   5   6   8   9   10

Did you notice there is not a #7 on the performance evaluation? You are working to be elite and extraordinary, instead of average and mediocre. Your evaluation may include, but is not limited to: your mindset – your focus – being goal-driven and purposeful – progression of skills – effort given – energy level – emotional regulation – getting outside of your comfort zone – using obstacles as an opportunity to grow – learning from your experience – helping others to get better.

DATE: M   T   W   TH   F   S   S

GHP PRINCIPLE: 3 THINGS I AM GRATEFUL FOR TODAY.

1.

2.

3.

NOTABLE DETAILS OF MY TRAINING/COMPETITION.

MY GOAL TODAY IS:

MY CONFIDENCE LEVEL IS:

         1   2   3   4   5
Low ←───→ High

MY INTERNAL PERFORMANCE STATE LEVEL IS:

1   2   3   4   5   6   7   8   9   10
Low Energy Level ←─────────────────────────→ High Energy Level

IDENTIFY/DESCRIBE SIGNAL LIGHTS I RECOGNIZED: Green – Yellow – Red

HOW DID I RELEASE MY YELLOW/RED LIGHTS?

Circle One: TRAINING DAY or COMPETITION DAY

WHAT DID I DO WELL TODAY? What Gets Rewarded Gets Repeated.

WHAT CAN I DO BETTER? The Struggle Is Necessary In Order To Learn, Grow, and Evolve.

HOW CAN I DO IT DIFFERENTLY? Keep It Super Simple. Be The Best At Getting Better.

TODAY I LEARNED THAT:

MY PERFORMANCE EVALUATION:

1   2   3   4   5   6   8   9   10

Did you notice there is not a #7 on the performance evaluation? You are working to be elite and extraordinary, instead of average and mediocre. Your evaluation may include, but is not limited to: your mindset – your focus – being goal-driven and purposeful – progression of skills – effort given – energy level – emotional regulation – getting outside of your comfort zone – using obstacles as an opportunity to grow – learning from your experience – helping others to get better.

DATE: M   T   W   TH   F   S   S

GHP PRINCIPLE: 3 THINGS I AM GRATEFUL FOR TODAY.

1.

2.

3.

NOTABLE DETAILS OF MY TRAINING/COMPETITION.

MY GOAL TODAY IS:

MY CONFIDENCE LEVEL IS:

```
        1            2            3            4            5
Low  ←———————————————————————————————————————————————————→  High
```

MY INTERNAL PERFORMANCE STATE LEVEL IS:

```
 1    2    3    4    5    6    7    8    9    10
Low Energy Level  ←——————————————————→  High Energy Level
```

IDENTIFY/DESCRIBE SIGNAL LIGHTS I RECOGNIZED: Green – Yellow – Red

HOW DID I RELEASE MY YELLOW/RED LIGHTS?

Circle One: TRAINING DAY or COMPETITION DAY

WHAT DID I DO WELL TODAY? What Gets Rewarded Gets Repeated.

WHAT CAN I DO BETTER? The Struggle Is Necessary In Order To Learn, Grow, and Evolve.

HOW CAN I DO IT DIFFERENTLY? Keep It Super Simple. Be The Best At Getting Better.

TODAY I LEARNED THAT:

MY PERFORMANCE EVALUATION:

1   2   3   4   5   6   8   9   10

Did you notice there is not a #7 on the performance evaluation? You are working to be elite and extraordinary, instead of average and mediocre. Your evaluation may include, but is not limited to: your mindset – your focus – being goal-driven and purposeful – progression of skills – effort given – energy level – emotional regulation – getting outside of your comfort zone – using obstacles as an opportunity to grow – learning from your experience – helping others to get better.

DATE: M T W TH F S S

GHP PRINCIPLE: 3 THINGS I AM GRATEFUL FOR TODAY.

1.

2.

3.

NOTABLE DETAILS OF MY TRAINING/COMPETITION.

MY GOAL TODAY IS:

MY CONFIDENCE LEVEL IS:

Low 1 2 3 4 5 High

MY INTERNAL PERFORMANCE STATE LEVEL IS:

1 2 3 4 5 6 7 8 9 10

Low Energy Level ← → High Energy Level

IDENTIFY/DESCRIBE SIGNAL LIGHTS I RECOGNIZED: Green – Yellow – Red

HOW DID I RELEASE MY YELLOW/RED LIGHTS?

Circle One: TRAINING DAY or COMPETITION DAY

WHAT DID I DO WELL TODAY? What Gets Rewarded Gets Repeated.

WHAT CAN I DO BETTER? The Struggle Is Necessary In Order To Learn, Grow, and Evolve.

HOW CAN I DO IT DIFFERENTLY? Keep It Super Simple. Be The Best At Getting Better.

TODAY I LEARNED THAT:

MY PERFORMANCE EVALUATION:

1   2   3   4   5   6   8   9   10

Did you notice there is not a #7 on the performance evaluation? You are working to be elite and extraordinary, instead of average and mediocre. Your evaluation may include, but is not limited to: your mindset – your focus – being goal-driven and purposeful – progression of skills – effort given – energy level – emotional regulation – getting outside of your comfort zone – using obstacles as an opportunity to grow – learning from your experience – helping others to get better.

DATE: .... M   T   W   TH   F   S   S

GHP PRINCIPLE: 3 THINGS I AM GRATEFUL FOR TODAY.

1.

2.

3.

NOTABLE DETAILS OF MY TRAINING/COMPETITION.

MY GOAL TODAY IS:

MY CONFIDENCE LEVEL IS:

Low 1 —— 2 —— 3 —— 4 —— 5 High

MY INTERNAL PERFORMANCE STATE LEVEL IS:

1   2   3   4   5   6   7   8   9   10
Low Energy Level ←————————————→ High Energy Level

IDENTIFY/DESCRIBE SIGNAL LIGHTS I RECOGNIZED: Green – Yellow – Red

HOW DID I RELEASE MY YELLOW/RED LIGHTS?

Circle One: TRAINING DAY or COMPETITION DAY

WHAT DID I DO WELL TODAY? What Gets Rewarded Gets Repeated.

WHAT CAN I DO BETTER? The Struggle Is Necessary In Order To Learn, Grow, and Evolve.

HOW CAN I DO IT DIFFERENTLY? Keep It Super Simple. Be The Best At Getting Better.

TODAY I LEARNED THAT:

MY PERFORMANCE EVALUATION:

1   2   3   4   5   6   8   9   10

Did you notice there is not a #7 on the performance evaluation? You are working to be elite and extraordinary, instead of average and mediocre. Your evaluation may include, but is not limited to: your mindset – your focus – being goal-driven and purposeful – progression of skills – effort given – energy level – emotional regulation – getting outside of your comfort zone – using obstacles as an opportunity to grow – learning from your experience – helping others to get better.

DATE: M   T   W   TH   F   S   S

GHP PRINCIPLE: 3 THINGS I AM GRATEFUL FOR TODAY.

1.

2.

3.

NOTABLE DETAILS OF MY TRAINING/COMPETITION.

MY GOAL TODAY IS:

MY CONFIDENCE LEVEL IS:

Low   1   2   3   4   5   High

MY INTERNAL PERFORMANCE STATE LEVEL IS:

1   2   3   4   5   6   7   8   9   10

Low Energy Level ⟵⟶ High Energy Level

IDENTIFY/DESCRIBE SIGNAL LIGHTS I RECOGNIZED: Green – Yellow – Red

HOW DID I RELEASE MY YELLOW/RED LIGHTS?

Circle One: TRAINING DAY or COMPETITION DAY

WHAT DID I DO WELL TODAY? What Gets Rewarded Gets Repeated.

WHAT CAN I DO BETTER? The Struggle Is Necessary In Order To Learn, Grow, and Evolve.

HOW CAN I DO IT DIFFERENTLY? Keep It Super Simple. Be The Best At Getting Better.

TODAY I LEARNED THAT:

MY PERFORMANCE EVALUATION:

1   2   3   4   5   6   8   9   10

Did you notice there is not a #7 on the performance evaluation? You are working to be elite and extraordinary, instead of average and mediocre. Your evaluation may include, but is not limited to: your mindset – your focus – being goal-driven and purposeful – progression of skills – effort given – energy level – emotional regulation – getting outside of your comfort zone – using obstacles as an opportunity to grow – learning from your experience – helping others to get better.

DAILY PERFORMANCE JOURNAL PAGES • **211**

DATE: M   T   W   TH   F   S   S

GHP PRINCIPLE: 3 THINGS I AM GRATEFUL FOR TODAY.

1.
2.
3.

NOTABLE DETAILS OF MY TRAINING/COMPETITION.

MY GOAL TODAY IS:

MY CONFIDENCE LEVEL IS:

        1   2   3   4   5
Low ←—————————————————————→ High

MY INTERNAL PERFORMANCE STATE LEVEL IS:

1   2   3   4   5   6   7   8   9   10
Low Energy Level ←—————————————→ High Energy Level

IDENTIFY/DESCRIBE SIGNAL LIGHTS I RECOGNIZED: Green – Yellow – Red

HOW DID I RELEASE MY YELLOW/RED LIGHTS?

Circle One: TRAINING DAY or COMPETITION DAY

WHAT DID I DO <u>WELL</u> TODAY? What Gets Rewarded Gets Repeated.

WHAT CAN I DO <u>BETTER</u>? The Struggle Is Necessary In Order To Learn, Grow, and Evolve.

<u>HOW</u> CAN I DO IT DIFFERENTLY? Keep It Super Simple. Be The Best At Getting Better.

TODAY I LEARNED THAT:

MY PERFORMANCE EVALUATION:

1   2   3   4   5   6   8   9   10

Did you notice there is not a #7 on the performance evaluation? You are working to be elite and extraordinary, instead of average and mediocre. Your evaluation may include, but is not limited to: your mindset – your focus – being goal-driven and purposeful – progression of skills – effort given – energy level – emotional regulation – getting outside of your comfort zone – using obstacles as an opportunity to grow – learning from your experience – helping others to get better.

MY NOTES

"Writing is another powerful way to sharpen the mental saw. Keeping a journal of our thoughts, experiences, insights, and learnings promotes mental clarity, exactness, and context."

—STEPHEN COVEY

"Start writing no matter what. The water does not flow until the faucet is turned on."

—LOUIS L'AMOUR

> *"Journal writing, when it becomes a ritual of transformation, is not only life-changing but life-expanding."*
>
> **—JENNIFER WILLIAMSON**

> *"The discipline of writing something down is the first step toward making it happen."*
>
> **—LEE IACOCCA**

"When you write things down, they sometimes take you places you hadn't planned."

—MELANIE BENJAMIN

> *"I think each of us can, through our writing, discover our super power."*
>
> **—DONALD MILLER**

"Fill your paper with the breathings of your heart."

—WILLIAM WORDSWORTH

"Documenting little details of your everyday life becomes a celebration of who you are."

—CAROLYN V. HAMILTON

"Keeping a journal of what's going on in your life is a good way to help you distill what's important and what's not."

—MARTINA NAVRATILOVA

"Writing in a journal reminds you of your goals and of your learning in life. It offers a place where you can hold a deliberate, thoughtful conversation with yourself."

—ROBIN S. SHARMA

"Have the courage to write whatever your dream is for yourself."

—MAY SARTON

"The simple act of writing down a goal and making a written plan for its accomplishment moves you to the top 3 percent."

—BRIAN TRACY

THINGS I CAN CONTROL vs THINGS I CANNOT CONTROL DRILL

"We are not born focusing. It's an acquired skill that requires initial effort and constant upgrading."

—ROBERT GENN

Things I Can Control vs. Things I Cannot Control Drill

This drill was one of the most important drills I have ever done. It shifted my perspective. It transformed how I trained, competed, and lived my life.

After I completed this drill, it opened up my mind and gave me momentum in developing the Elite Mindset I needed, in order to win a World Championship.

The goal of this drill is to first list all the **Things You Cannot Control** in your life. Be specific. Details matter.

Next, list all the **Things You Can Control** in your life. Be specific. Details matter.

The first time I did this drill was with my Mental Performance Coach. My list of **"Things I Cannot Control"** went on and on. It was easy for me to identify all of the things out of my control.

After I finished my extremely long list, my coach asked me, **"What Can You Control?"** I never thought about what I could control. I was at a loss for answers. There was a lengthy pause. Finally, I said, "I can control when I start my event and when I finish."

My Coach began to ask me questions such as, "Can you control your **appearance, attitude, preparation, positive self-talk, energy, effort?**" I responded, "Yes" to each of those.

I began to connect the dots. My list of **Things I Can Control** grew exponentially. I realized I had a lot more control of my life than I initially believed I did.

The **prize** in doing this exercise is identifying how much of your day you FOCUS on **Things You Cannot Control vs. Things You Can Control.**

> **Elite athletes focus 80% of their time on things they can control and focus 20% of their time on things they cannot control.**

The first step in performance change is awareness. This drill is an awareness drill. Once you have the awareness your focus can be better, you have the power to make the shift and do better.

The following is a mix and match starter list of, **Things I Can Control, and Things I Cannot Control.** They are in no particular order. The spirit of providing this list is to help spark you with ideas, as you complete this transformational drill for yourself.

This is the first drill you want to complete. As you progress in your mental performance journey revisit this drill and rework it on the next page.

Your Perspective – The Weather – Your Patience – Spectators – Conditions – Your Process – Other Competitors – What Other People Think, Say, and Feel About You – The Officials – Your Time/Score – The Announcer – Noise – The Past – The Future – The Present – Your Thoughts – The Outcome/Results – Your Enthusiasm – Parents – Your Focus – Your Equipment – Traffic – Coaches – Your Mindset – Taking A Breath – Your Response – Your Routine – Your Decisions and Choices

THINGS I CANNOT CONTROL	**THINGS I CAN CONTROL**

Percentage of Time I Focus on Things I Cannot Control: _____ %

Percentage of Time I Focus on Things I Can Control: _____ %

THINGS I CANNOT CONTROL	**THINGS I CAN CONTROL**

Percentage of Time I Focus on Things I Cannot Control: _____ **%**

Percentage of Time I Focus on Things I Can Control: _____ **%**

RECOGNIZING SIGNAL LIGHTS DRILL

*"You must be in control of yourself
before you can control your performance."*

—DR. KEN RAVIZZA

Recognizing Signal Lights

As I was running down my World Championship, there was always adversity headed in my direction. If life was easy breezy, going my way, and I was getting the results I wanted, I knew it would be a matter of time before things shifted. This is life. No one gets a free pass from challenges, distractions, struggles, failures, or adversity. The **Recognizing Signal Lights Drill** is foundational in helping you perform at your optimal level no matter what the circumstance.

The more you invest into training awareness of your Yellow and Red Signal Lights the faster you will become at recognizing them. The faster you recognize them the more proficient you'll become in releasing Yellow and Red Lights.

The more you train awareness of your Green Signal Lights, the more proficient you'll become in refocusing and performing on a Green Light.

Gaining awareness of your Yellow and Red Signal Lights does not mean you will never again experience them. However, it does mean you will not be held back by them. You can take action to release them and get back on a Green Light. Being on a Green Light means you are in control of yourself and that gives you the opportunity to perform at your optimal level.

"Don't dwell on what went wrong. Instead, focus on what to do next. Spend your energies on moving forward finding the answer."
- **DENIS WAITLEY**

In my book, ***Heart of a Champion,*** I share in detail about my Signal Lights and my Release – Refocus Routines. Here is brief description of how to execute Release and Refocus Routines.

The Yellow and Red Signal Light **Release Routine** is a 3-Step Process:
1. Take a nice, deep breath on a focal point.
2. Do a physical action and attach an association to it. The association gives meaning to why you are doing it.
3. Say a verbal trigger(s). Keep them process based, productive, positive, and in the present moment.

See the bottom of page 28 for an example of this 3-Step Release.

The Green Signal Light **Refocus Routine** is a 2-Step Process:
1. Take a nice, deep breath on a focal point.
2. Execute a predetermined thought, image, and/or feeling that reaffirms you are ready to perform at your optimal level.

I invite you to review the following page where I share a few personal examples of my Green, Yellow, and Red Signal Lights.

SHOW AND TELL PAGE

6 WAYS TO RECOGNIZE SIGNAL LIGHTS

"I AM IN CONTROL"	"I AM LOSING CONTROL"	"I HAVE LOST CONTROL"

GREEN LIGHT	YELLOW LIGHT	RED LIGHT

Identify what is my body language like:

Big Body Language. Looking people in the eye.	Small Body Language. Looking down - Arms folded.	Defeated Body Language. Closed Off from Others.

Identify where is my focus:

On Things I Can Control. Present Moment.	Past Mistakes. On Feelings and Emotions.	Blaming & Complaining. My Results/Future Outcome.

Identify what does my self-talk sound like:

Positive & Productive. Process Based.	Negative & Unproductive. Outcome Based.	Believing the Negative. Being an Inner Critic/Bully.

Identify how does my body feel:

Energized. Strong.	Tight Jaw - Tight Body. Shoulders Hiked.	Extremely Low Energy. Panic, Anxiety, or Extremely Excited.

Identify what is my perspective:

I Get To Do This! I Am Grateful To Be Here!	I Have To Be Here. Hoping I Don't Mess Up.	I Need to Win or Playing Not to Lose. I Don't Belong Here.

Identify what is the situation/what is going on:

I Am Trusting My Routines and Process. I Am in Control of My Emotions.	I Am Not Getting the Results I Want. I Am Speeding Up My Process.	I Am Crying. I Want To Quit.

Identify what is my body language like:

Green Light:

Yellow Light:

Red Light:

Identify where is my focus:

Green Light:

Yellow Light:

Red Light:

Identify what does my self-talk sound like:

Green Light:

Yellow Light:

Red Light:

Identify how does my body feel:

Green Light:

Yellow Light:

Red Light:

Identify what is my perspective:

Green Light:

Yellow Light:

Red Light:

Identify what is the situation/what is going on:

Green Light:

Yellow Light:

Red Light:

CONFIDENCE CONDITIONING STATEMENTS DRILL

"Whether you believe you can or you believe you can't—you're right."

—HENRY FORD

Confidence Conditioning Statements

> *"Your beliefs become your thoughts,*
> *Your thoughts become your words,*
> *Your words become your actions,*
> *Your actions become your habits,*
> *Your habits become your values,*
> *Your values become your destiny."*
> **—MAHATMA GANDHI**

I want to challenge you to press your pause button for a moment and reflect on how you speak to yourself. You may be thinking, "I do not talk to myself." This is the exact little voice inside your mind that I am referring too.

Words are powerful. They come from what's in your mind and heart. Should you be curious to know where you will be in your life five years from today, I encourage you to listen to how you talk to yourself right now. What does your self-talk sound like? Are you a great ally or big enemy to yourself? Are you a world class coach or a cynic critic towards yourself? Is your self-talk negative, unproductive, belittling, and demeaning? Or is your self-talk positive, productive, and elevating, focusing on what you can do and what you want to have happen?

While reflecting, ask yourself, "Is how I speak to myself helping me or hindering me in becoming the best at getting better?"

Negative self-talk and word choices hinder mindset. Did you know what you think about and talk about most of the time is who you will become?

The one thing that I did which shifted my mindset from average to an elite mindset did not cost any money, it took no special talent on my part, and it required less than a ten-minute investment each day. This strategy transformed my life in a positive direction. The one thing was how I spoke to myself and changing the words I used every single day.

The following drill is how you can implement this one thing in your life.

A few times throughout the day schedule time to pause for a minute or two. Speak positive, energetic, productive, empowering and process-based, confidence conditioning statements to yourself internally or out loud. To reinforce this strategy more deeply, add speaking confidence statements with a meaningful physical action.

I have provided some of my own personal **Confidence Conditioning Statements** that may get you started in doing this drill. A physical action that I have used begins with smiling and taking a full breath before stating each **Confidence Conditioning Statement**. Then, I will either place my hand over my heart or tap my chest while I say and savor each and every one of the statements. All the while, I am visualizing myself as the person I want to be. In doing this, it changed how I began to show up for myself. This strategy was a turning point for the type of relationship I began building with myself. I was filling up my own confidence tank. This was the start of becoming someone I had never known before.

Changing the words I used took intentional, daily focus. I began to pay attention to my intention of using words that would catapult me forward toward my Bold Goals, instead of casting me back into mediocrity. Word by word I began building a championship vocabulary. I vowed to eliminate words from my vocabulary that hindered the new mindset I was intentionally building.

The following is a sampling of words I have eliminated and the replacement words I choose to use instead.

Eliminate:	Spend	–	I'm spending time training, spending time doing homework, or spending time with my family.
Replace with:	Invest	–	I'm investing time training, investing time doing homework, and investing time with my family! (When investing time, you expect an ROI – return on your investment.)
Eliminate:	Have To	–	I have to train, have to go to school, and have to go to work. I have to compete.
Replace with:	Get To	–	I get to train, get to go to school, or get to go to work!
Eliminate	Slump	–	I am in a slump. Why me? This is awful!
Replace with:	Challenged	–	I am being challenged! This is an opportunity to grow!
Eliminate:	Loser	–	I am a loser. I lost, again. I do not belong here!
Replace with:	Learner	–	I am a learner! I'm learning from my mistakes!
Eliminate:	Don't	–	Don't be nervous. Don't eat junk food.
Replace with:	What I Want	–	What I want is to breathe and stay relaxed! What I want is to eat like a World Champion!
Eliminate:	Worry	–	I am worried about what may happen.
Replace with:	Focus	–	I am focused on what I can control and what I want to have happen!

Eliminate:	**Nervous**	–	I'm nervous about competing. What if I make a mistake? I am feeling too much pressure.
Replace with:	**Excited**	–	I'm excited to be competing! What will I learn? I am grateful. I enjoy doing this!
Eliminate:	**Failure**	–	I did not get the result I desired. I failed. I am a failure.
Replace with:	**Feedback**	–	I am gathering feedback and data! I can do it differently next time!
Eliminate:	**Can't**	–	I can't do it. I don't want to do it. I quit!
Replace with:	**Yet**	–	I am not able to do it, YET! I am figuring this out!
Eliminate:	**Need**	–	I need to win. This is it, it's now or never!
Replace with:	**Want**	–	I want to win! This is fun! I am trusting my training.
Eliminate:	**Perfection**	–	I am striving for perfection. I have to train/perform perfectly.
Replace with:	**Progression**	–	I am focused on my progression, taking my next step forward! I will be the best at getting better!
Eliminate:	**Just and Only**	–	I am just a Breakaway Roper. I only have a 2-horse bumper pull trailer. (Please do not minimize who you are, what you have, what you are doing, and what you want.)
Replace with:	**The Facts**	–	I am a Breakaway Roper! I have a 2-horse bumper pull trailer! (Insert your sport, event, or position. Insert a piece of equipment that you have that is not the best, but you are making the best of what you have.)

We are all much more alike than we are different. We all want more in life. In order to have more, you must become more. What you say to yourself, how you say it, and the words you choose are greatly important in who you will become and what you will do.

I want to encourage you to continue building your championship vocabulary and championship mindset by working this next drill daily. I invite you to review the following page, where I share some of my personal statements.

SHOW AND TELL PAGE
CONFIDENCE CONDITIONING STATEMENTS

★ I am brave, courageous, and bold in everything I do.

★ I am motivated, disciplined, and committed to my Bold Goals.

★ I always perform with big body language and confidence.

★ I choose to focus on the positive, the present, and my next best move.

★ I trust my routines and perform in the moment.

★ I am prepared and ready to perform.

★ I am worthy, loved, and enough in all circumstances.

★ I am focusing on my process over the outcome.

★ I am a winner and a learner.

★ I am breathing in confidence and exhaling determination.

★ I am breathing in focus and exhaling positivity.

★ I am grateful for this opportunity to perform my best.

★ I do hard, difficult, and challenging things really, really, well.

★ Today is going to be a great day, and I am ready to perform at my optimal level.

★ Obstacles make me stronger — Bring it on!

★ I am letting go of mistakes and choosing to refocus.

★ I am exactly where I need to be in my journey and enjoying this moment.

★ I control what I can control and let go of what I can't.

Now it's your turn! Use the following 6 pages to complete this drill for yourself.

CONFIDENCE CONDITIONING STATEMENTS

ARE YOU STUCK? UNCERTAIN WHERE TO START? REVIEW PAGES 248 – 251 FOR IDEAS.

★
★
★
★
★
★
★
★
★
★
★
★
★
★
★
★
★
★
★
★

CONFIDENCE CONDITIONING STATEMENTS

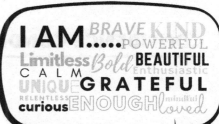

★

★

★

★

★

★

★

★

★

★

★

★

★

★

★

★

★

★

★

CONFIDENCE CONDITIONING STATEMENTS

I AM positive, joyful, adaptable, caring, lovable, authentic, spiritual, helpful, productive, trustworthy, prepared, purposeful, hard working, persistent, blessed, mindful, healthy, amazing

★
★
★
★
★
★
★
★
★
★
★
★
★
★
★
★
★
★
★

CONFIDENCE CONDITIONING STATEMENTS

★
★
★
★
★
★
★
★
★
★
★
★
★
★
★
★
★
★
★
★

CONFIDENCE CONDITIONING STATEMENTS

I AM positive, joyful, adaptable, caring, lovable, authentic, spiritual, helpful, productive, trustworthy, prepared, purposeful, hard working, persistent, healthy, blessed, mindful, amazing

★
★
★
★
★
★
★
★
★
★
★
★
★
★
★
★
★
★
★

CONFIDENCE CONDITIONING STATEMENTS

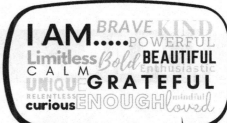

- ★
- ★
- ★
- ★
- ★
- ★
- ★
- ★
- ★
- ★
- ★
- ★
- ★
- ★
- ★
- ★
- ★
- ★
- ★
- ★

I AM...

- VALUABLE
- PATIENT
- TRUSTING
- COMPASSIONATE
- PASSIONATE
- BLESSED
- LOVING
- FIERCE
- PRESENT
- MINDFUL
- POWERFUL
- DETERMINED
- RESOURCEFUL
- TRANSFORMING
- GROWING
- FUN
- EVOLVING
- EMPATHETIC
- PHENOMENAL
- ENERGIZED
- ENTHUSIASTIC
- HEALTHY
- OPEN MINDED
- CALM
- CENTERED
- COMPOSED
- BALANCED
- BREATHING
- EXTRAORDINARY

I AM...

- RAISING MY LEVEL OF TRAINING AND HABITS
- EXACTLY WHERE I NEED TO BE
- ENJOYING THIS MOMENT
- AN OVERCOMER
- CHOOSING TO MAKE GREAT CHOICES
- LOCKED IN
- GAINING THE RIGHT STRATEGIES
- PUTTING IN THE MASSIVE TIME
- MOVING FORWARD
- DOING THE WORK
- ATTAINING A GROWTH MINDSET
- EMBRACING ADVERSITY & CHALLENGES
- AWESOME AT DOING HARD THINGS
- PURPOSEFUL WHEN I TRAIN
- OPEN TO FEEDBACK
- SETTING NEW BENCHMARKS
- FOLLOWING THROUGH ON MY SET INTENTIONS
- LOOKING FORWARD TO MAKING MISTAKES BECAUSE THIS IS HOW I LEARN AND GET BETTER
- CONTROLLING WHAT I CAN CONTROL
- EXACTLY WHERE I NEED TO BE
- ENJOYING THIS MOMENT

I AM...

- A FOUNTAIN
- A PROBLEM SOLVER
- A SCIENTIST IN MY LABORATORY CONDUCTING AN EXPERIMENT
- IN CHARGE OF MYSELF
- RESPONSIBLE OF HOW I RESPOND
- TAKING A NICE, DEEP BREATH
- BLESSED TO BE HERE
- RIGHT WHERE I WANT/NEED TO BE
- LOVING WHAT I DO AND DOING WHAT I LOVE
- FOCUSED ON THE PRESENT MOMENT
- FOCUSED ON WHAT'S IMPORTANT NOW
- LOOKING FORWARD TO THIS
- SEEING THIS AS A CHALLENGE
- BEING CHALLENGED
- EXPECTING GREAT THINGS TO HAPPEN
- LOVING THE PROCESS
- TRUSTING THE PROCESS
- TRUSTING MY HORSE
- TRUSTING MY PREPARATION
- TRUSTING MYSELF
- TRAINING ONE DAY AT A TIME
- TRUSTING MY INSTINCTS
- TRUSTING MY INTUITION

I AM...

- SMART
- GRATEFUL
- RELAXED
- INSPIRATIONAL
- FORGIVING
- FOCUSING
- PROACTIVE
- HOPEFUL
- SUPPORTED
- FASCINATED
- LIMITLESS
- SUCCESSFUL
- CAPABLE
- IMPROVING
- FASCINATED
- DISCIPLINED
- PREPARED
- READY
- INTENSE
- TRUTHFUL
- EXCITED
- GENUINE
- UNIQUE
- RELENTLESS
- DRIVEN
- COMPETING
- CENTERED
- COMFORTABLE
- INTUITIVE

I AM...

- WILLING TO DO EXTRA
- LETTING GO OF MISTAKES
- IN CONTROL OF MY THOUGHTS
- CHOOSING TO REFOCUS
- IN CONTROL OF MY EMOTIONS
- CHOOSING TO REDIRECT MY THOUGHTS
- CHOOSING TO BE POSITIVE
- IN CONTROL OF MY MIND AND MY BODY
- ENJOYING LIFE
- LOVING THE JOURNEY
- THE AUTHOR OF MY OWN STORY
- OWNING MY MISTAKES
- EMBRACING HARD THINGS
- KEEPING MY PROCESS GREATER THAN THE OUTCOME
- STEPPING UP AND STEPPING OUT
- ABLE TO DO THIS
- WANTING TO DO THIS
- ASKING FOR HELP
- COMPETING WITH MY COMPETITORS
- COMMITED TO MY BOLD GOALS
- DOING MY BEST
- CHANGING EVERY DAY
- LOVING MYSELF UNCONDITIONALLY

I AM...

- EMBRACING THE SUCK
- COMPETING WITH CONVICTION
- COMPETING WITH CONFIDENCE
- BELIEVING IN MYSELF
- FAILING FORWARD
- RAISING MY BASEMENT
- JUICEFUL (JACKED UP INTENSE CONTAGIOUS ENERGY)
- USING MY FAILURE AS FUEL
- DOING MY BEST
- RUNNING DOWN MY BOALD GOAL
- FINDING A WAY
- FIGURING IT OUT
- SAYING, "SO WHAT, GET BETTER"
- SAYING, "SO WHAT, DO BETTER"
- SAYING, "SO WHAT, DON'T MATTER"
- CHEERING MYSELF ON
- COMPETING WITH MYSELF
- CHOOSING TO BE CHEERFUL AND HAPPY
- GOING ALL IN AND GOING ALL OUT
- WORKING MY PROCESS TO THE BEST OF MY ABILITY
- LOCKED INTO MY PROCESS
- SEEKING OUT SOLUTIONS
- LETTING GO OF THE THINGS I CANNOT CONTROL
- DOING BIG BODY LANGUAGE
- FOCUSING ON WHAT'S IMPORTANT NOW (WIN)
- TRUSTING MY TRAINING

CONFIDENCE CONDITIONING STATEMENTS DRILL

I AM...

- RESILIENT
- CURIOUS
- INDEPENDENT
- A BADCAT
- INTELLIGENT
- BRIGHT
- CLEVER
- SINCERE
- SETTING NEW BENCHMARKS
- CHEERING MYSELF ON
- CONSISTENT
- AWARE
- EAGER
- HONEST
- FAIR
- HOPEFUL
- CONFIDENT
- PRODUCTIVE
- GENUINE
- POSSIBLE
- REFOCUSING
- BOLD
- COURAGEOUS
- ELITE
- REFLECTING
- TRUSTWILLING
- APPRECIATIVE
- A CHAMPION
- EMPOWERED

I AM...

- BIGGER THAN ANY OBSTACLE
- AN ENERGY GIVER
- GETTING BETTER EVERY DAY
- IMPROVING EVERY DAY
- THE CHANGE
- IN CHARGE OF MYSELF
- GIVING 100% OF WHAT I HAVE EVERY DAY
- SHOWING UP FOR MYSELF EVERY DAY
- ACTING DIFFERENTLY THAN HOW I FEEL
- FOCUSING ON WHAT I CAN CONTROL
- CHOOSING WHO I BECOME
- HAVING FUN
- GIVING FULL EFFORT
- USING MY FAILURES AS A STEPPING STONE
- USING MY FAILURES AS FERTILIZER
- LAUGHING AT MYSELF
- NOURISHING MY MIND/BODY WITH NOURISHING THOUGHTS
- RESPECTFUL OF MYSELF
- IN CHARGE OF HOW I FEEL
- TAKING ACTION
- TAKING ACTION RIGHT NOW
- DOING IT NOW
- MAKING IT HAPPEN

I AM...

- GATHERING DATA
- CONDUCTING AN EXPERIMENT
- THINKING NEUTRAL THOUGHTS
- SPIRALING UP
- THINKING PRODUCTIVE THOUGHTS
- TALKING PRODUCTIVE TALK
- FOCUSING ON THE DETAILS
- THINKING OUTSIDE THE BOX
- I AM DOUBLING DOWN ON MY EFFORT
- TRAINING CONSISTENTLY
- FALLING IN LOVE WITH THE PROCESS
- DOING WHAT IT TAKES FOR AS LONG AS IT TAKES
- DIGGING DEEPER
- DOING IMPORTANT WORK
- COMPETING ONE RUN AT A TIME
- TRAINING ONE RUN AT A TIME
- RUNNING A RACE WITH NO FINISH LINE
- THE BEST AT GETTING BETTER
- THE BEST AT RUNNING MY RACE
- THE BEST AT WORKING HARD AND WORKING SMART
- THE BEST AT BEING MYSELF
- MORE THAN WHAT I DO
- MORE THAN WHAT I WIN

I AM...

- AMBITIOUS
- COMPETENT
- QUICK
- CREATIVE
- BRAVE
- CARING
- ADAPTABLE
- A WARRIOR
- BRAINSTORMING
- ANTI-FRAGILE
- PERSISTENT
- FAITHFUL
- ACCOUNTABLE
- TRUSTWORTHY
- POSITIVE
- KIND
- FRIENDLY
- WINNING
- ENCOURAGING
- AUTHENTIC
- A WINNER
- LOYAL
- HUMBLE
- STRONG
- MENTALLY TOUGH
- HELPING OTHERS
- A FIERCE COMPETITOR
- MASTERING MY SKILLS
- DOING PHENOMENAL WORK

I AM...

- LETTING IT HAPPEN
- LETTING GO OF MISTAKES
- LETTING GO OF ERRORS
- LETTING GO OF NEGATIVITY
- FOCUSED ON PROGRESSION
- IDENTIFYING & REMOVING OBSTACLES
- SHUTTING THE GATE ON MY NEGATIVE THOUGHTS AND EMOTIONS
- USING BIG BODY LANGUAGE
- IN MY OPTIMAL PERFORMANCE STATE
- RESPONSIBLE FOR PERFORMING AT MY PEAK PERFORMANCE STATE
- RESPONSIBLE FOR MY RESPONSE
- IN CONTROL OF MY RESPONSE
- SMILING AT OBSTACLES
- SAYING, "BRING IT ON!"
- SAYING, "OBSTACLES MAKE ME STRONGER."
- BELIEVING IN MYSELF
- GIVING IT MY ALL
- THINKING LIKE A CHAMPION
- WORKING LIKE A CHAMPION
- REFLECTING ON MY PERFORMANCE
- DOING HARD THINGS REALLY WELL
- LOOKING FOR THE GOOD

I AM...

- TRAINING WITH A PURPOSE
- MAKING STRONG DECISIONS
- DOING THE IMPOSSIBLE
- DOING EXTRA WORK
- AT PEACE
- TRAINING WITH A PURPOSE
- KEEPING BOTH EYES ON MY PROCESS
- MOVING FORWARD
- LEVELING UP
- LIVING IN THE MOMENT
- IN THE MOMENT
- RELEASING NEGATIVE THOUGHTS
- RELEASING YELLOW/RED SIGNAL LIGHTS
- COMPETING ONE EVENT AT A TIME
- COMPETING WITH MYSELF
- COMPETING ONE DAY AT A TIME
- COMPETING ONE ROUND AT A TIME
- BETTER TODAY THAN I WAS YESTERDAY
- RESPONSIBLE TO FILL MY CONFIDENCE TANK
- MAKING ONE RUN AT A TIME
- EXECUTING MY SUCCESS CHECKLIST DAILY
- BELIEVING I'M A CHAMPION
- SEEKING OPPORTUNITIES TO GET OUTSIDE MY COMFORT ZONE
- REVERSE ENGINEERING AND EXECUTING MY PLAN

IDENTIFYING MY GREATNESS A – Z DRILL

"Knowing yourself is the beginning of all wisdom."

—ARISTOTLE

Identifying My Greatness From A – Z

Directions: This is a Confidence Building drill. The goal is to identify your current strengths, valuable characteristics, and productive traits that are already inside of you. Choose 2 words, that begin with each letter of the alphabet that describe the greatness inside of you.

For example:
A – Ambitious and Altruistic
B – Big Body Language and Brave
C – Confident and Courageous

Invest time reflecting and reviewing your answers. You may want to read them to yourself or better yet, read them out loud. Greatness is inside of you. You are not lacking anything.

Self-confidence is an inside job. Your confidence is a you and you deal. Results do not define your confidence. What other people think, say, do or feel about you does not define your confidence.

Confidence is a choice. Choose to do confidence.

A

B

C

D

E

F

G

H

I

J

K

CONTINUED

L

M

N

O

P

Q

R

S

T

U

V

W

X

Y

Z

FANTASTIC WORK COMPLETING THIS DRILL!

Celebrating your strengths will build and boost your confidence.

Developing unshakable confidence can be uncomfortable work. It may bubble up self-limiting beliefs such as thinking others will perceive you as being arrogant or cocky.

This is not the spirit of this confidence-building drill. Its purpose is to help you gain awareness of your strengths. Your strengths are not fixed. You can develop your strengths.

I want to challenge you to continue developing your strengths.

BUILDING A CONFIDENCE RESUME DRILL

"Remind yourself what you've been through and what you've had the strength to endure."

—MARCUS AURELIUS

Building A Confidence Resume

You may have already written a resume that highlights your life experiences, such as your education/training, skills, and achievements. The goal of that type of resume is to land an interview with those who can help you achieve the next step in what you are targeting.

In much the same vein, I have invested time in the routine of writing what I call a **Confidence Resume.** Building a **Confidence Resume** is very empowering because it highlights key experiences I have had along the way, in my journey. All the things I record help me remember the challenges, struggles and adversities that I have grown through. It also sparks me to celebrate my accomplishments, victories, wins, goal setting and goal getting. The **Confidence Resume's** purpose is to showcase you— to you! My **Confidence Resume** moments began when I was young girl in South Dakota, and they continue to this very day. The time of year I write varies, and some years I have written more than one.

Because being confident is an "inside" job, I compare it to having a confidence fuel tank. Just as you fill your vehicle with fuel, before you leave for an event, you must also fill your confidence fuel tank. Receiving compliments and getting awards, titles, money, and recognition all help build confidence; however, those things are akin to the "regular grade" fuel that goes into your confidence fuel tank. That kind of fuel gets you down the road, but it won't give you the power you need to travel up the mountain of adversity or through the valley of struggles and mistakes. Being intentional about recording each experience, the good, the bad, and when the stuff hits the fan, will help fill your confidence fuel tank with premium, high-octane fuel. That premium fuel will get you up those mountains of adversity and through the valleys of despair. It will light the fire inside of you to bounce back up quickly and grow through those experiences. Premium, high-octane fuel in your confidence fuel tank will power you toward your **Bold Goals** with consistent momentum.

Your life's journey is a compilation of all your experiences. As I share in my book, ***Heart of a Champion***, it's the journey, and who you become in the process, that is the true prize. Examining each experience carefully reveals what you learned, how you grew, relationships you built, and who you have become, on your journey. Your **Confidence Resume** is a collection of all the things that have helped you become a better version of you.

GET STARTED TODAY!

To begin the **Confidence Resume** exercise, you will need a quiet space and an open mind. Start by taking a few nice, deep breaths, and be ready to embrace the greatness that is inside of you. This can be emotional, or not. However, having tissues nearby may be a good idea. The goal of this exercise is to reflect, identify, unpack, and write down experiences which have grown you during your journey. Completing the **Confidence Resume** allows you to revisit life-shaping experiences and fill up your tank!

The following list includes the **Confidence Resume** prompts that are included in this drill. Go all-in, unpacking each of the courageous, challenging, fantastic, phenomenal, beautiful, and amazing things you have done throughout your journey.

- Identified and built on my strengths
- Overcame and grew through challenges, struggles, and adversities
- Said, "YES," before I had it all figured out
- Listened to and trusted my intuition
- Earned trust moments with myself by doing what I said I would do
- Failed beautifully and turned it into an opportunity to grow
- Invested resources in myself
- Gave 100% of what I had, knowing I didn't have 100% to give
- Treated myself like my best friend amidst fumbles, mistakes, and failure
- Stepped outside my comfort zone
- Accomplished specific goals
- Noteworthy accomplishments, victories, and wins
- Took action steps toward my goals
- Cultivated and nurtured relationships
- Helped someone along in their journey

Complete the **Confidence Resume** with a spirit of celebration. Celebrate each and every one of the items you write down. Why? Because what gets rewarded, gets repeated!

The goal is to repeat more of these experiences because they each fill your confidence fuel tank with high octane fuel and provide you with optimal growth opportunities. I encourage you to review your **Confidence Resume** throughout the year.

Many times, you may take what you do and how you do it for granted. Each of these writing prompts is meant to encourage you and give you courage, shifting your perspective of taking what you do and how you do it *as granted*. I absolutely, positively, 100% guarantee you do hard, difficult, challenging, fearful, uncomfortable things, really well. I am inviting you to own your greatness.

Did you know that it takes between 1 billion to 3.3 billion of years for natural diamonds to form. The process begins a hundred miles below the earth's surface. It takes extreme heat and extreme pressure for this phenomenal and amazing transformation to take place and without it, there would not be any diamonds in the world. Just like diamonds are beautiful, unique, and highly sought-after precious stones; building your **Confidence Resume** is how you will dig deep and uncover your diamonds.
Go find your diamonds!

LET'S DO THIS!

IDENTIFY MY STRENGTHS.

 Reflect: *What can I do to level up my strengths?*
Strengths are not fixed. You can make your strengths better.

Identify them all: physical attributes, strength and conditioning, intellectual, mental mindset, emotional, spiritual, relationships, financial, elite inner circle, core principles, skills and skill sets.

> *"Sometimes we're tested not to show our weaknesses, but to discover our strengths."*
> **– UNKNOWN**

IDENTIFY 3-5 EXPERIENCES WHEN I HAVE BEEN CHALLENGED AND OR EXPERIENCED ADVERSITY.

 Reflect: *How did I overcome? What skills did I use to overcome? What are the lessons and learns I gained from growing through the challenge or adversity?*

Challenges and adversity are always coming. No one gets a free pass from them. You have the ability to choose how you respond.

> E + R = O
> (Event + Response = Outcome)
> *"If you don't like your Outcomes change your Responses."*
> **— JACK CANFIELD**

IDENTIFY FEAR DOORS I HAVE WALKED THROUGH.

 Reflect: *How did I do it being scared? What are the strategies I used? How did I tap into my courage to take action?*

Fear Doors are things that "scare the dickens of you" but your next step forward is on the other side.

> *"I learned that courage was not the absence of fear, but the triumph over it. The brave man is not he who does not feel afraid, but he who conquers that fear."*
> **– NELSON MANDELA**

IDENTIFY EXPERIENCES WHEN I SAID YES, BEFORE I HAD IT ALL FIGURED OUT OR HAD A PLAN IN PLACE. *THIS IS CALLED "READY, FIRE, AIM!"*

Reflect: *What did I learn? How did the decision to "Ready, Fire, Aim!" help me to move forward?*

"Ready. Fire. Aim. Do it! Make it happen! Action counts. No one ever sat their way to success."
—**TOM PETERS**

IDENTIFY EXPERIENCES WHERE I LISTENED TO AND TRUSTED MY INTUITION.

 Reflect: *What did I learn? How did the decision of listening to and then trusting my intuition help me to move forward?*

"If prayer, is you talking to God, then intuition is God talking to you."
—DR. WAYNE DYER

IDENTIFY "DO WHAT YOU SAY YOU WILL DO" MOMENTS (DWYSYWD).

Reflect: *How will I increase my DWYSYWD Moments?*

DWYSYWD is incredibly important to fill your confidence tank. DWYSYWD for yourself is how you develop trust with yourself. The Latin root of confidence is "intense trust in oneself."

Here is a short-list that may get you started: commit to a nutrition plan—stay disciplined in a strength and conditioning plan—consistently follow your success checklist—flourish relationships – train each day purposefully with a goal to get better – stay committed to your Bold Goals.

IDENTIFY MY "FAILED BEAUTIFULLY" MOMENTS.

 Reflect: *What did I learn from my "Failed Beautifully" moments? How did I turn them into opportunities to grow?*

You can learn valuable lessons from your "Failed Beautifully" moments. These moments may include painful embarrassment, epic fails, or catastrophe. You may have learned that you did not die; the sun still came back up; your elite inner circle is still there to help you and cheer you on to take your next step forward.

IDENTIFY MOMENTS WHERE I MADE THE DECISION TO INVEST IN MYSELF.

💡 **Reflect:** *How can I continue to invest in myself?*

Resources that you may want to invest into may include time, training, coaching, effort, money, sweat, rest, and recovery. Investing in yourself, doing the work needed to fill your tank, allows you to have more to give others. You cannot give what you do not have.

IDENTIFY WHEN I HAVE GIVEN 100% OF WHAT I HAD, KNOWING I DID NOT HAVE 100% TO GIVE.

💡 **Reflect:** *How did I dig deeper and tap into my reserve tank?*

Acting differently than how you feel is a Superpower. You can develop this Superpower by training it.

> *"Your actions change your attitudes. Your motions change your emotions. Your movements change your moods."*
> **—DR. ROBERT GILBERT**

IDENTIFY WHEN I HAVE PRACTICED KINDNESS, CARING, EMPATHY, FORGIVENESS, HUMOR, AND NON-JUDGMENT WITH MYSELF.

 Reflect: *How can I give myself more Grace? How can I be my own best friend, instead of a big bully? How can I be my own best cheerleader, instead of an inner critic?*

Commit to treating yourself like you treat your friends.

> *"Treat yourself like you would someone you're responsible for helping."*
> **– JORDAN B. PETERSON**

IDENTIFY WHEN I HAVE STEPPED OUTSIDE OF MY COMFORT ZONE.

 Reflect: *How can I intentionally and consistently make a practice of getting outside of my comfort zone?*

Here is a short-list of what it may look like to get outside of your comfort zone: asking for help —doing something for the first time—being the odd person out—not following the crowd—being told you can't do it and doing it anyway – having the courage to do what challenges and or scares you. – running down your Bold Goals.

IDENTIFY GOALS I HAVE ACCOMPLISHED.

Reflect: *How did I accomplish my goals? What champion characteristics did I practice consistently to help me stay motivated, disciplined, and committed?*

Here is a short-list of champion characteristics to get you started: building an elite inner circle—asking for help—looking for solutions—being positive and productive with your thoughts, talk, and actions—hard work—smart work—extra work—bouncing back up from adversity—training with a purpose – developing and training your grit.

IDENTIFY MY ACCOMPLISHMENTS, VICTORIES, WINS.

 Reflect: *What did the pathway to my success look like? Is there a common denominator of how I did it? How did I execute my plan?*

Success leaves clues. Every step counts, and every step matters. How you do anything is how you do everything. Keeping building your *Championship Playbook*!

> *"Success is no accident. It is hard work, perseverance, learning, studying, sacrifice, and most of all, love of what you are doing or learning to do."*
> **– PELÉ**

IDENTIFY AND CELEBRATE ACTION STEPS I HAVE TAKEN TOWARD MY GOALS.

 Reflect: *Reverse engineer the action steps I will take over the next 3 months that will move me toward my goals.*

The one thing that shifts goal setting to goal getting is ACTION. I want to encourage you to be courageous and take consistent action toward what fills your heart and lights your soul on fire.

> *"You don't have to be great to start, but you have to start to be great."*
> **– ZIG ZIGLAR**

IDENTIFY RELATIONSHIPS I HAVE CULTIVATED AND NURTURED. IDENTIFY HOW I HAVE HELPED OTHERS IN THEIR JOURNEY.

Reflect: *How can I continue to build my powerful and empowering inner circle? How can I continue to help others rundown what they are working towards?*

You become the average of the 5 people who you surround yourself with the most. Seek out and find people who align with your core principles, demonstrate a growth mindset, and have achieved what you want. Choose people who celebrate you and want you to succeed!

"You can have everything in life you want, if you will just help other people get what they want."
—ZIG ZIGLAR

BUILDING A SUCCESS CHECKLIST DRILL

"You'll never change your life until you change something you do daily. The secret of your success is found in your daily routine."

— JOHN C. MAXWELL

Building A Success Checklist

Building a **Success Checklist** and executing on it consistently have been a foundational strategy in helping me optimize my performance and run down my Bold Goals. I absolutely, positively, 100% guarantee, it will do the same for you!

A **Success Checklist** is a compilation of important intentions you have identified, that when doing them daily or for a specified number of times during the week, it helps you to perform your optimal best, day in and day out.

Aligning your daily intentions with your Bold Goals is how you make big things happen.

The four step **Success Checklist** process is as follows:

1. **Set** your intentions for the tasks you want to prioritize on your **Success Checklist**.
2. **Schedule** your intentions. Identify the day, time of day, and number of times per week you will execute on your set intentions.
3. **Measure** your intentions. Gather, document, and evaluate data. Set new benchmarks to mark your progress. Reward your consistency by marking off each task as you complete it.
4. **Reflect and Refocus** on your set intentions. What did you do well? What can you do better? How can you do it differently? What are you learning?

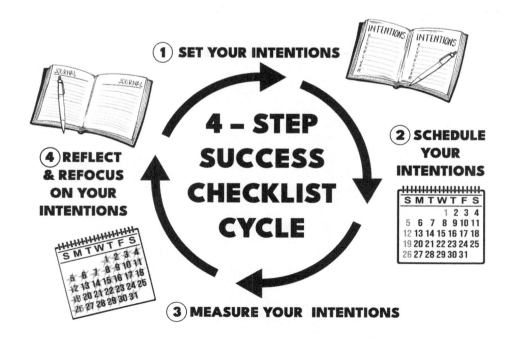

Your **Success Checklist** will allow you to seize momentum and perform your optimal best when it matters most. I created the **Success Checklist** acronym: **REV UP 2 JAM**. Each of these nine letters represent an intention that I include on my **Success Checklist**. This has proven to help me perform at an elite level in all arenas of my life. I am inviting you to use the following monthly **Success Checklist** journaling pages to build your daily habits and routines of excellence. The following **REV UP 2 JAM** acronym is an explanation of my **Success Checklist**. Executing on these nine intentions catapults me to show up at my optimal level consistently and it will do the same for you.

REV UP 2 JAM

KEEP YOUR COMMITMENT TO YOUR DAILY HABITS AND ROUTINES

READ I commit to reading 5-10 pages every day in morning. I commit to listening to an audiobook throughout each day as well.

EXERCISE I commit to strength training 2 days a week. I commit to conditioning training 2 days a week. I commit to active recovery, stretching, flexibility, and balance training 3 days a week.

VISUALIZE I commit to visualization training every day of the week, at a minimum of three times a day: Before I get out of bed in the morning, prior to training, before I fall asleep at night. Visualization is a great drill to implement as it helps fill your confidence fuel tank.

UNIQUE I commit to at least one activity that is outside-of-the-box thinking for a minimum of 90 days. This intention helps you gain an edge over the competition. This intention is something most people will not be willing to do. When you commit to this activity for at least 90 days you will level up: building new skills and establishing better habits. Here are a few of my examples: Working one-on-one with a Mental Performance Coach, Running Coach, Strength Coach, Nutrition Coach, Vision Performance Coach, Breathwork Coach. Learned to ride a balance board while implementing skills from my sport. Learned to juggle.

PRODUCTIVE Every day when I wake up, I commit to telling myself, "Today is going to be a great day!" I put my hand on my heart and tell myself, "I love myself." I've set the intention for my day to be productive. Being productive is not being busy and marking things off of a do-to list. Being productive is accomplishing what you have intentionally decided to make a priority. You get to choose your perspective, positive talk and thoughts, persistence, patience, process, and preparation. You get to choose to live moment to moment being present. Choosing to live PRODUCTIVELY is how you seize the momentum, optimize performance, and spiral up consistently.

DOUBLE DOWN

2 I commit to doubling down on at least one intention every day for at least 90 days. Extra work is where I am able to take bold steps forward toward my Bold Goals. Committing to this intention for 90 days gives you the opportunity to establish better habits and level up. Here are a few of my doubling down examples: meditation, visualization, reading, workouts, increasing my protein for muscle growth, training specific skills and skill sets for my sports.

JOURNAL I commit to Journaling every day of the week. I split my journaling into 2 parts: morning and evening. Research supports that putting pen to paper is beneficial in helping you accomplish what you are working towards. Journaling helps to give more organization, clarity, creativity, and reflection to your thought processes.

I AM WORTHY, FOCUSED, PREPARED, LOVED

AFFIRMATIONS I commit to writing and saying out loud 5-10 positive affirmations every day in the morning and throughout the day. Affirmations and Confidence Conditioning Statements fill your confidence fuel tank with high-octane fuel.

MEDITATE I commit to meditating every day in the morning for a minimum of 10 minutes. The benefits I receive from meditating greatly exceeded my expectations. Here are few of the benefits I receive from meditating: lowered anxiety, increased happiness, falling asleep faster, exercising more, increased mindfulness, the opportunity to perform optimally during a variety of pressure-filled situations. I encourage you to be open-minded and get curious about implementing meditation into your daily routine.

You may have the mindset that **Building A Success Checklist** sounds like a great drill however, it would be extremely difficult to fit this drill into your day.

If this is your mindset, please consider this: How difficult will it be to compete with someone who does build a **Success Checklist** and you don't?

Implementing this drill is an investment you make into yourself. I compare it to the flight attendant who gives the airplane safety instructions of putting on your own oxygen mask first before you help someone else. Taking care of yourself allows you to not only help others, but rundown what means the most to you.

The following are 5 strategies that will help you get started and dominate this drill.

- Start by setting one or two intentions on your **Success Checklist**. You get to choose how much time you want to invest into your intention. Begin this drill setting intentions that are easy to accomplish even on a day that is fast, furious, and the stuff hits the fan.
- You have the most control of your day first thing in the morning and before bedtime. Both of these times are great opportunities to implement your set intentions.
- Adopting the perspective that doing this drill is an opportunity instead of another obligation.
- Eliminate "All or Nothing Thinking." When you do not have the best day, accomplish what you can. Strive for your best in the moment, instead of perfection.
- Take the "Pillow Test" every night. As you rest your head on the pillow at night ask yourself this question: Am I glad I did, or do I wish I would have worked my **Success Checklist**?" Taking the "Pillow Test" is a great strategy to help hold yourself accountable and find a way to get it done.

The more you work your **Success Checklist**, the more you will like it and the better you will become at it.

SUCCESS CHECKLIST

STEP ONE: Set your intentions for the tasks you want to prioritize on your Success Checklist.

                                                                                              MONTH   /   **YEAR**

★ Read every day 7/7 — Finish the Alchemist and re-read Champion's Mind. Take Notes.

★

★

★

★

★

★

★

★

★

★

★

★

★

★

★

SUCCESS CHECKLIST TRACKER

STEP TWO: Schedule your intentions. Identify the day, time of day, and number of times per week you will execute on your set intentions.

STEP THREE: Measure your intentions. Reward your consistency by marking off each task as you complete it.

> List your Success Checklist intentions and goals on the following lines below. Note how many times during the week you will commit to this action. __/7

Month _____

> Color in the corresponding square for each day you keep your commitment to your Success Checklist intentions and goals. Measurement Is Motivation!!

Read 10 pages every day at 6 am.   7/7 ■■■■■■■□□□□□□□□□□□□□□□□□□□□□□□□

STEP FOUR: Reflect and Refocus on your set intentions. What did you do well? What can you do better? How can you do it differently? Use your Daily Performance Journaling Pages.

BUILDING A SUCCESS CHECKLIST DRILL • **281**

SUCCESS CHECKLIST

STEP ONE: Set your intentions for the tasks you want to prioritize on your Success Checklist.

                                                                                 /

                                                          MONTH   **YEAR**

★ _____

★ _____

★ _____

★ _____

★ _____

★ _____

★ _____

★ _____

★ _____

★ _____

★ _____

★ _____

★ _____

★ _____

★ _____

★ _____

★ _____

SUCCESS CHECKLIST TRACKER

STEP TWO: Schedule your intentions. Identify the day, time of day, and number of times per week you will execute on your set intentions.

STEP THREE: Measure your intentions. Reward your consistency by marking off each task as you complete it.

List your Success Checklist intentions and goals on the following lines below. Note how many times during the week you will commit to this action. __/7

Month

Color in the corresponding square for each day you keep your commitment to your Success Checklist intentions and goals. Measurement Is Motivation!!

1 2 3 4 5 6 7 8 9 10 11 12 13 14 15 16 17 18 19 20 21 22 23 24 25 26 27 28 29 30 31

.... __/7 ☐☐☐☐☐☐☐☐☐☐☐☐☐☐☐☐☐☐☐☐☐☐☐☐☐☐☐☐☐☐☐
.... __/7 ☐☐☐☐☐☐☐☐☐☐☐☐☐☐☐☐☐☐☐☐☐☐☐☐☐☐☐☐☐☐☐
.... __/7 ☐☐☐☐☐☐☐☐☐☐☐☐☐☐☐☐☐☐☐☐☐☐☐☐☐☐☐☐☐☐☐
.... __/7 ☐☐☐☐☐☐☐☐☐☐☐☐☐☐☐☐☐☐☐☐☐☐☐☐☐☐☐☐☐☐☐
.... __/7 ☐☐☐☐☐☐☐☐☐☐☐☐☐☐☐☐☐☐☐☐☐☐☐☐☐☐☐☐☐☐☐
.... __/7 ☐☐☐☐☐☐☐☐☐☐☐☐☐☐☐☐☐☐☐☐☐☐☐☐☐☐☐☐☐☐☐
.... __/7 ☐☐☐☐☐☐☐☐☐☐☐☐☐☐☐☐☐☐☐☐☐☐☐☐☐☐☐☐☐☐☐
.... __/7 ☐☐☐☐☐☐☐☐☐☐☐☐☐☐☐☐☐☐☐☐☐☐☐☐☐☐☐☐☐☐☐
.... __/7 ☐☐☐☐☐☐☐☐☐☐☐☐☐☐☐☐☐☐☐☐☐☐☐☐☐☐☐☐☐☐☐
.... __/7 ☐☐☐☐☐☐☐☐☐☐☐☐☐☐☐☐☐☐☐☐☐☐☐☐☐☐☐☐☐☐☐
.... __/7 ☐☐☐☐☐☐☐☐☐☐☐☐☐☐☐☐☐☐☐☐☐☐☐☐☐☐☐☐☐☐☐
.... __/7 ☐☐☐☐☐☐☐☐☐☐☐☐☐☐☐☐☐☐☐☐☐☐☐☐☐☐☐☐☐☐☐
.... __/7 ☐☐☐☐☐☐☐☐☐☐☐☐☐☐☐☐☐☐☐☐☐☐☐☐☐☐☐☐☐☐☐
.... __/7 ☐☐☐☐☐☐☐☐☐☐☐☐☐☐☐☐☐☐☐☐☐☐☐☐☐☐☐☐☐☐☐
.... __/7 ☐☐☐☐☐☐☐☐☐☐☐☐☐☐☐☐☐☐☐☐☐☐☐☐☐☐☐☐☐☐☐
.... __/7 ☐☐☐☐☐☐☐☐☐☐☐☐☐☐☐☐☐☐☐☐☐☐☐☐☐☐☐☐☐☐☐
.... __/7 ☐☐☐☐☐☐☐☐☐☐☐☐☐☐☐☐☐☐☐☐☐☐☐☐☐☐☐☐☐☐☐
.... __/7 ☐☐☐☐☐☐☐☐☐☐☐☐☐☐☐☐☐☐☐☐☐☐☐☐☐☐☐☐☐☐☐

STEP FOUR: Reflect and Refocus on your set intentions. What did you do well? What can you do better? How can you do it differently? Use your Daily Performance Journaling Pages.

SUCCESS CHECKLIST

STEP ONE: Set your intentions for the tasks you want to prioritize on your Success Checklist.

.... / ....
MONTH   YEAR

★ ....

★ ....

★ ....

★ ....

★ ....

★ ....

★ ....

★ ....

★ ....

★ ....

★ ....

★ ....

★ ....

★ ....

★ ....

★ ....

★ ....

SUCCESS CHECKLIST TRACKER

STEP TWO: Schedule your intentions. Identify the day, time of day, and number of times per week you will execute on your set intentions.

STEP THREE: Measure your intentions. Reward your consistency by marking off each task as you complete it.

> List your Success Checklist intentions and goals on the following lines below. Note how many times during the week you will commit to this action. __/7

Month ....

> Color in the corresponding square for each day you keep your commitment to your Success Checklist intentions and goals. Measurement Is Motivation!!

1 2 3 4 5 6 7 8 9 10 11 12 13 14 15 16 17 18 19 20 21 22 23 24 25 26 27 28 29 30 31

.... __/7 ☐☐☐☐☐☐☐☐☐☐☐☐☐☐☐☐☐☐☐☐☐☐☐☐☐☐☐☐☐☐☐
.... __/7 ☐☐☐☐☐☐☐☐☐☐☐☐☐☐☐☐☐☐☐☐☐☐☐☐☐☐☐☐☐☐☐
.... __/7 ☐☐☐☐☐☐☐☐☐☐☐☐☐☐☐☐☐☐☐☐☐☐☐☐☐☐☐☐☐☐☐
.... __/7 ☐☐☐☐☐☐☐☐☐☐☐☐☐☐☐☐☐☐☐☐☐☐☐☐☐☐☐☐☐☐☐
.... __/7 ☐☐☐☐☐☐☐☐☐☐☐☐☐☐☐☐☐☐☐☐☐☐☐☐☐☐☐☐☐☐☐
.... __/7 ☐☐☐☐☐☐☐☐☐☐☐☐☐☐☐☐☐☐☐☐☐☐☐☐☐☐☐☐☐☐☐
.... __/7 ☐☐☐☐☐☐☐☐☐☐☐☐☐☐☐☐☐☐☐☐☐☐☐☐☐☐☐☐☐☐☐
.... __/7 ☐☐☐☐☐☐☐☐☐☐☐☐☐☐☐☐☐☐☐☐☐☐☐☐☐☐☐☐☐☐☐
.... __/7 ☐☐☐☐☐☐☐☐☐☐☐☐☐☐☐☐☐☐☐☐☐☐☐☐☐☐☐☐☐☐☐
.... __/7 ☐☐☐☐☐☐☐☐☐☐☐☐☐☐☐☐☐☐☐☐☐☐☐☐☐☐☐☐☐☐☐
.... __/7 ☐☐☐☐☐☐☐☐☐☐☐☐☐☐☐☐☐☐☐☐☐☐☐☐☐☐☐☐☐☐☐
.... __/7 ☐☐☐☐☐☐☐☐☐☐☐☐☐☐☐☐☐☐☐☐☐☐☐☐☐☐☐☐☐☐☐
.... __/7 ☐☐☐☐☐☐☐☐☐☐☐☐☐☐☐☐☐☐☐☐☐☐☐☐☐☐☐☐☐☐☐
.... __/7 ☐☐☐☐☐☐☐☐☐☐☐☐☐☐☐☐☐☐☐☐☐☐☐☐☐☐☐☐☐☐☐
.... __/7 ☐☐☐☐☐☐☐☐☐☐☐☐☐☐☐☐☐☐☐☐☐☐☐☐☐☐☐☐☐☐☐
.... __/7 ☐☐☐☐☐☐☐☐☐☐☐☐☐☐☐☐☐☐☐☐☐☐☐☐☐☐☐☐☐☐☐
.... __/7 ☐☐☐☐☐☐☐☐☐☐☐☐☐☐☐☐☐☐☐☐☐☐☐☐☐☐☐☐☐☐☐
.... __/7 ☐☐☐☐☐☐☐☐☐☐☐☐☐☐☐☐☐☐☐☐☐☐☐☐☐☐☐☐☐☐☐

STEP FOUR: Reflect and Refocus on your set intentions. What did you do well? What can you do better? How can you do it differently? Use your Daily Performance Journaling Pages.

BUILDING PERFORMANCE ROUTINES DRILL

*"The way you train reflects
the way you perform."*

—DONENE TAYLOR

Building Performance Routines

Identifying your **Performance Routines** and being disciplined, committed and consistent in executing them is key in giving yourself the best opportunity to perform at your optimal level. I break down **Performance Routines** into 3 parts. I use the visual of an old-fashioned hourglass to describe them. See the diagram below.

The top half of the hourglass represents your Pre-Performance Routine. The middle, the smallest part of the hourglass, represents your Performance Routine. The bottom half of the hourglass represents your Post Performance Routine. Investing time writing in your Performance Journal is an important part of your Post Performance Routine.

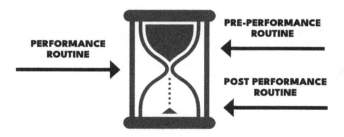

In my book, *Heart of a Champion,* I write about the first time I was asked to write out each of my 3 Performance Routines: Pre-Performance, Performance, Post Performance. I was respectful to my Mental Performance Coach; however, in my mind I was thinking, "I don't need to write out my Performance Routines. I know what to do, and I've been doing this for a long time."

I can tell you with conviction I never regretted doing this extremely important work. It took time, effort, and some revisions, but writing out my **Performance Routines**, physical and mental, was a game changer. This drill instantly elevated how I began to show up for myself and perform.

One of the benefits I received after I dialed in my performance routines was the consistency in my performance. Consistency in my performance was a foundational piece that I was missing for decades.

What I learned from building, writing, and committing to this work was this:
- If you cannot describe your process, then you don't have a process.
- In order to trust your process, then you must have a process to trust.

Should you be curious to know how detailed my **Performance Routines** are you can find them in my book, *Heart of a Champion*.

> *"It's the little details that are vital. Little things make big things happen."*
> **– JOHN WOODEN**

SPORT/EVENT/POSITION:

PRE-PERFORMANCE ROUTINE

SPORT/EVENT/POSITION:

PERFORMANCE ROUTINE

SPORT/EVENT/POSITION:

POST PERFORMANCE ROUTINE

SPORT/EVENT/POSITION:

PRE-PERFORMANCE ROUTINE

SPORT/EVENT/POSITION:

PERFORMANCE ROUTINE

SPORT/EVENT/POSITION:

POST PERFORMANCE ROUTINE

SPORT/EVENT/POSITION:

PRE-PERFORMANCE ROUTINE

SPORT/EVENT/POSITION:

PERFORMANCE ROUTINE

SPORT/EVENT/POSITION:

POST PERFORMANCE ROUTINE

TECHNICAL PERFORMANCE AND MENTAL PERFORMANCE BASIC SKILLS DRILL

*"World class performers do the basics the best.
Be the best at getting better."*

—DONENE TAYLOR

Technical Performance and Mental Performance Basic Skills

> *"If you always do what you have always done, you'll always get what you always got."*
> — **HENRY FORD**

I have a sign of success in my barn that invites me to stay off the unproductive, insanity loop. My SOS reads, "If you change nothing, nothing will change."

In theory, this is easy to understand, but if you don't have the awareness of what needs to change or how to change it, then that task will be very difficult. The following **Technical Performance and Mental Performance Basic Skills Drill** is how I began to make transformational change in all arenas of life.

Technical Performance Skills help you develop the physical movement and motions necessary to perform at your sport, event, and/or position. These skills are trained by performing drills and repetitive movements. The way in which you train greatly determines how well you perform. Training at different speeds, including a variety of scenarios and pressure situations, help you develop the skill sets needed to perform optimally in a variety of situations.

Mental Performance Skills help you to develop an elite mindset. This includes developing a growth mindset, confidence, focus, positive self-talk, emotional regulation, and your ability to bounce-back up after experiencing adversity. Developing your mental skills help you become the best at getting better because you embrace a learner's mindset in everything you do.

Developing your **Technical Performance Skills and Mental Performance Skills** concurrently gives you an edge to become an optimal performer in your sport, event, and/or position.

You may find, while working this drill, you bridge the gap between:

- Your confidence and competence,
- How you train and in how you compete,
- The action steps you are taking now and the Bold Goals you want to achieve.

The goal, as you consistently execute this drill, is to exponentially level up your skill sets of technical and mental performance. One thing all world class performers have in common is that they mastered the basics and have made a fierce and disciplined commitment to remaster the basics every single day.

When running down Bold Goals, every step counts and every step matters. Drills build skills. Skills develop skill sets.

This drill helps you identify basic skills, set a current benchmark, develop strategies, and take immediate, consistent action needed to perform at your optimal level.

When you adopt the mindset that you treasure all of your disciplined work, including your blood, sweat and tears, then you will treasure each resource you've invested into your Bold Goal, and you will measure it all. Remember, measurement is motivation.

I encourage you to implement this drill with an open mind. Spark your best beginner's mindset. **Think Basic. Think Simple. Think Process. Think Strategically. Think Patience.**

This drill requires you to be creative, get curious, ask questions, and break down your performance into basic skills. You may want to discuss with and get feedback from your coach/mentor/role models.

Identify your benchmark for each basic skill as a "strength" or as a "needs work." Be honest with yourself. This is a self-awareness drill that will be instrumental in helping you level up your performance. When you intentionally do the work to make your "strengths" stronger and your "needs work" better, you gain momentum and level up your performance exponentially.

I encourage you to invest time identifying *why* and *how* you do what you do for each basic skill. Gaining a deep understanding of each basic skill and executing consistent training helps build your confidence. This confidence comes from you believing in and owning your process. Trusting your process allows you to obtain a realistic benchmark of your performance. When you trust your process, you compete your best in all different situations and scenarios. Trusting your process allows you perform at your optimal level.

I use this drill to help develop and plan, purposeful and deliberate training sessions. This is an important part of my playbook that gives me an edge in reverse engineering my Bold Goals and closing the gap from where I am to where I want to go.

I invite you to review the following pages, as I share a snapshot of how I use this drill.

Included are multiple journaling pages for you to create and customize your **Technical Performance and Mental Performance Basic Skills.**

> *"Bold Goals get achieved one step at a time. Consistent self-evaluation of your performance gives you the assurance that you are traveling in the right direction."*
> **—DONENE TAYLOR**

SHOW AND TELL PAGE

1. Identify & List the Technical Performance Basic Skills that help you to perform optimally in your event/sport.
2. Identify each skill as a "Strength" or as a "Needs Work" for yourself.
3. Identify why and how you do what you do for each skill. Identify drills to build each skill. Develop mantras.

SPORT/EVENT/POSITION: Breakaway Roping

TECHNICAL PERFORMANCE BASIC SKILLS	STRENGTH	NEEDS WORK	IDENTIFY WHY & HOW YOU DO WHAT YOU DO FOR EACH SKILL. IDENTIFY DRILLS TO BUILD EACH SKILL. DEVELOP MANTRAS.
1. Grip the Rope Correctly	✓		Adjust rope when it shifts in my hand. Slow motion drill. Feel rope leaving my fingers.
2. Feed the Rope	✓		Daily benchmark drill. "Feed the rope toward the target."
3. Balance - Angle - Momentum		✓	Train each day with Shadow Swings. End the day roping in the dark. "Feel It and Trust It."
4. Keep Arms Bent & Together		✓	Continue to train as I ride/warm-up. Watch TB video. Train roping dummy & sled. Imitate Drill.
5. Swing Positions 1-2-3-4		✓	Visualize each swing position — forward & reverse. Train in the dark on dummy. "#4 Shut the door." Slow-motion drill.
6. Turn the Rope Over		✓	Break rope over at target. Overcompensate Drill. Slow-motion drill. Video. Mirror Drill.
7. Feel the Tip of the Rope		✓	Have the rope in my hand minimally 90 minutes a day. Make the rope an extension of myself. Rope in the dark. Visualize.
8. Swing Rope Around the Neck		✓	D-GAD Delivery #4 position. Be intentional to keep my rope on the right side. "Nothing Changes."
9. Deliver Rope with Both Hands	✓		"My left hand follows my right hand." Video and respond to feedback. Shadow Drills, Dummy Drills, Visualize.
10. Pull Slack	✓		Follow rope to the target drill on dummy. Imitate Drill.
11. Distribute weight: 50% Feet/ 50% Seat		✓	Shadow Work Drills while riding. Ride Balance Board. Train My Balance 5/7 days.
12. Correct Leg & Feet Position		✓	"My heels are under my butt. My knees are over my toes. My chest is over my knees." Video training session/respond to feedback.
13. Correct Upper Body Position		✓	Do core exercises 5/7 days. Be intentional engaging my core all day long! Train to Compete.
14. Ride Into the Box		✓	Execute my Performance Routines. Breathe, flip my switch, trust my training. Process focused. Timing & Tempo.
15. Always Score Something		✓	"Be Still" when the chute bangs open. Have a goal of what to score before I ride into the box. Execute my plan during runs.
16. Leave the Corner: Keep Left Arm Bent - Melt in Saddle - Be on Feet		✓	Continue to train while roping sled & shadow work. Visualize & Video. Train to Compete.
17. Focus & Crossover Behind Calf		✓	Continue eye exercises. Bright markers on calf to heighten my focus. Overcompensate Drill. Live Runs.
18. Pace the Calf Under the Rope		✓	Implement opened-eyed visualization drills while riding. Change up speed & energy while riding horse.
19. Reel Calf In		✓	Implement Shadow Training and Slow-Motion Training. Focus keeping a relaxed shoulder. "Find Calf - Reel In." Imitate Drill.
20. Stop Horse Straight & Turn Horse Into the Rope		✓	Shadow and Live Drills while riding at different speeds. Execute proper lower leg, seat, body, hand position.

SHOW AND TELL PAGE

1. Identify & List the Mental Performance Basic Skills that help you to perform optimally in all arenas of your life.
2. Identify each as a "Strength" or as a "Needs Work" for yourself.
3. Identify why and how you do what you do for each skill. Identify drills to build each skill. Develop mantras.

MENTAL PERFORMANCE BASIC SKILLS	STRENGTH	NEEDS WORK	IDENTIFY WHY & HOW YOU DO WHAT YOU DO FOR EACH SKILL. IDENTIFY DRILLS TO BUILD EACH SKILL. DEVELOP MANTRAS.
1. Anti-Fragility	✓		Strength is in the struggle. "Bring it on!" Look for opportunities to get uncomfortable & bounce-back up quickly.
2. Breathing - Relaxing - Meditation	✓		Continue to build my Relaxation Response. Execute Drills 3x a day. "Always be where my feet are."
3. Champion/Growth Mindset	✓		Live into "Above The Line" Championship Principles. Continue to work FT program. Complete homework daily.
4. Confidence		✓	Continue to look for opportunities to take action before I am ready. "Trust My Training." Ready, Fire, Aim." Get it on my calendar.
5. Daily Habits & Routines		✓	Continue to plan out my week on Sunday. "What gets scheduled gets done."
6. Emotional Regulation	✓		Continue to channel my inner scientist. Gather data and information. "Feelings are not facts."
7. Focus	✓		Level Up my scores on my concentration and focusing drills.
8. Goal Setting & Goal Getting	✓		Reverse Engineer microscope and telescope goals. Set Benchmarks. Focus on process and progression. "My goal must be in my control."
9. Journaling	✓		Performance Journal. Reflect - Refocus - Perform - WIN.
10. Leadership, Culture & Principles	✓		Transformational Leadership. "Good Vibes Only" Focus Principles: Autotelic, Mastery, & Empowerment.
11. Motivation	✓		Stay energized! Schedule targeted benchmarks. Double Down on My Why. "How bad do I want it?" "I Get to!"
12. Nutrition & Hydration		✓	Measure my MACROS & water intake daily. "Measurement is Motivation."
13. Performance Routines	✓		Timing, tempo, & speed drill. Focus on consistency.
14. Preparation & Training	✓		Give full effort with energy & enthusiasm every single day. "Progression not perfection."
15. Productive Self-Talk & Thoughts	✓		Bead Drill - get new benchmark. CART Drill. Say it & feel it drill – 3x a day. "Words are powerful!"
16. Reading	✓		Continue to read 10 pages per day. Listen daily to an audio book. "Leaders are readers."
17. Recognizing Signal Lights - Release - Refocus	✓		Continue to gain awareness of signal lights. Release yellow/red signal lights. Check-In Drill.
18. Sleep & Active Recovery		✓	8 hours Sleep/night. Walk path 4/7 days. Foam Roller 7/7 days. Take care of myself so I can give more to others.
19. Strength & Conditioning		✓	Schedule extra strength training each week. Implement Legs/Back drills to mirror TD event.
20. Visualization & Mental Imagery	✓		Visualize Vividly 2-3 times per day. "See it. Feel it. Trust it. Love it." Make a new highlight video reel.

TECHNICAL PERFORMANCE BASIC SKILLS

SPORT/EVENT/POSITION: _____

	STRENGTH	NEEDS WORK	IDENTIFY WHY & HOW YOU DO WHAT YOU DO FOR EACH SKILL. IDENTIFY DRILLS TO BUILD EACH SKILL. DEVELOP MANTRAS.
1.			
2.			
3.			
4.			
5.			
6.			
7.			
8.			
9.			
10.			
11.			
12.			
13.			
14.			
15.			
16.			
17.			
18.			
19.			
20.			

MENTAL PERFORMANCE BASIC SKILLS

	STRENGTH	NEEDS WORK	IDENTIFY WHY & HOW YOU DO WHAT YOU DO FOR EACH SKILL. IDENTIFY DRILLS TO BUILD EACH SKILL. DEVELOP MANTRAS.
1.			
2.			
3.			
4.			
5.			
6.			
7.			
8.			
9.			
10.			
11.			
12.			
13.			
14.			
15.			
16.			
17.			
18.			
19.			
20.			

TECHNICAL PERFORMANCE BASIC SKILLS

SPORT/EVENT/POSITION:

	STRENGTH	NEEDS WORK	IDENTIFY WHY & HOW YOU DO WHAT YOU DO FOR EACH SKILL. IDENTIFY DRILLS TO BUILD EACH SKILL. DEVELOP MANTRAS.
1.			
2.			
3.			
4.			
5.			
6.			
7.			
8.			
9.			
10.			
11.			
12.			
13.			
14.			
15.			
16.			
17.			
18.			
19.			
20.			

MENTAL PERFORMANCE BASIC SKILLS

	STRENGTH	NEEDS WORK	IDENTIFY WHY & HOW YOU DO WHAT YOU DO FOR EACH SKILL. IDENTIFY DRILLS TO BUILD EACH SKILL. DEVELOP MANTRAS.
1.			
2.			
3.			
4.			
5.			
6.			
7.			
8.			
9.			
10.			
11.			
12.			
13.			
14.			
15.			
16.			
17.			
18.			
19.			
20.			

TECHNICAL PERFORMANCE BASIC SKILLS

SPORT/EVENT/POSITION: ....

	STRENGTH	NEEDS WORK	IDENTIFY WHY & HOW YOU DO WHAT YOU DO FOR EACH SKILL. IDENTIFY DRILLS TO BUILD EACH SKILL. DEVELOP MANTRAS.
1.			
2.			
3.			
4.			
5.			
6.			
7.			
8.			
9.			
10.			
11.			
12.			
13.			
14.			
15.			
16.			
17.			
18.			
19.			
20.			

MENTAL PERFORMANCE BASIC SKILLS

	STRENGTH	NEEDS WORK	IDENTIFY WHY & HOW YOU DO WHAT YOU DO FOR EACH SKILL. IDENTIFY DRILLS TO BUILD EACH SKILL. DEVELOP MANTRAS.
1.			
2.			
3.			
4.			
5.			
6.			
7.			
8.			
9.			
10.			
11.			
12.			
13.			
14.			
15.			
16.			
17.			
18.			
19.			
20.			

TECHNICAL PERFORMANCE BASIC SKILLS

SPORT/EVENT/POSITION: ....

	STRENGTH	NEEDS WORK	IDENTIFY WHY & HOW YOU DO WHAT YOU DO FOR EACH SKILL. IDENTIFY DRILLS TO BUILD EACH SKILL. DEVELOP MANTRAS.
1.			
2.			
3.			
4.			
5.			
6.			
7.			
8.			
9.			
10.			
11.			
12.			
13.			
14.			
15.			
16.			
17.			
18.			
19.			
20.			

MENTAL PERFORMANCE BASIC SKILLS

	STRENGTH	NEEDS WORK	IDENTIFY WHY & HOW YOU DO WHAT YOU DO FOR EACH SKILL. IDENTIFY DRILLS TO BUILD EACH SKILL. DEVELOP MANTRAS.
1.			
2.			
3.			
4.			
5.			
6.			
7.			
8.			
9.			
10.			
11.			
12.			
13.			
14.			
15.			
16.			
17.			
18.			
19.			
20.			

BUILDING A WHOOP PERFORMANCE GRID DRILL

"If it's important to you, WHOOP IT! Actually, WHOOP E-V-E-R-Y-T-H-I-N-G!"

—DONENE TAYLOR

Building A WHOOP Performance Grid

I complete a **WHOOP Performance Grid** before I train and compete. I **WHOOP** important phone calls, meetings, and speaking presentations. If it is important to me, **I WHOOP it first!**

W   Identifying exactly what you **WANT** to have happen brings clarity of purpose.

H   Understanding **HOW** you will achieve what you want helps you focus.

O   Setting the intention of the **OUTCOME** you want gives you a target to aim toward.

O   Being realistic and open to identifying **OBSTACLES** allows you to be proactive and solution focused.

P   Developing a **PLAN,** before a plan is needed, gives you confidence and peace of mind to perform at your optimal level.

I want to encourage you to incorporate the **WHOOP Performance Grid** as part of your Pre-Performance Routine. You may want to review the **Building Performance Routines Drill,** beginning on page 287, to learn more.

The **WHOOP Performance Grid** puts power and control in your hands, as you train and compete. Completing a **WHOOP Performance Grid** empowers you to organize your thoughts and gives you a process to work. Even when stuff hits the fan or goes off the rails, you are in control of how you will respond. It is in your hands what you will learn, how you will grow, and the next, best step you will take.

Investing time completing **WHOOP Performance Grids** is an investment that you are making in yourself.

Remember, anytime you make an investment you expect a return on your investment. The return of investment you receive will be in the form of progression. The progression of closing the gap from where you are to where you want to go is the goal.

WHOOP PERFORMANCE GRID

W What do I **WANT**: ....
....

H **HOW** will I do it: ....
....

O **OUTCOME** I will experience: ....
....

O **OBSTACLES** I may encounter: ....
....

P **PLAN** to work/grow through the obstacles: ....
....

W What do I **WANT**: ....
....

H **HOW** will I do it: ....
....

O **OUTCOME** I will experience: ....
....

O **OBSTACLES** I may encounter: ....
....

P **PLAN** to work/grow through the obstacles: ....
....

WHOOP PERFORMANCE GRID

W What do I **WANT**: ....

H **HOW** will I do it: ....

O **OUTCOME** I will experience: ....

O **OBSTACLES** I may encounter: ....

P **PLAN** to work/grow through the obstacles: ....

W What do I **WANT**: ....

H **HOW** will I do it: ....

O **OUTCOME** I will experience: ....

O **OBSTACLES** I may encounter: ....

P **PLAN** to work/grow through the obstacles: ....

WHOOP PERFORMANCE GRID

W What do I **WANT:** ....

H **HOW** will I do it: ....

O **OUTCOME** I will experience: ....

O **OBSTACLES** I may encounter: ....

P **PLAN** to work/grow through the obstacles: ....

W What do I **WANT:** ....

H **HOW** will I do it: ....

O **OUTCOME** I will experience: ....

O **OBSTACLES** I may encounter: ....

P **PLAN** to work/grow through the obstacles: ....

WHOOP PERFORMANCE GRID

W What do I **WANT**: ....
....

H **HOW** will I do it: ....
....

O **OUTCOME** I will experience: ....
....

O **OBSTACLES** I may encounter: ....
....

P **PLAN** to work/grow through the obstacles: ....
....

W What do I **WANT**: ....
....

H **HOW** will I do it: ....
....

O **OUTCOME** I will experience: ....
....

O **OBSTACLES** I may encounter: ....
....

P **PLAN** to work/grow through the obstacles: ....
....

EQUIPMENT AND ESSENTIAL SUPPLY INVENTORY

*"Expect the best.
Prepare for the unexpected.
Perform with your whole heart."*

—DONENE TAYLOR

Equipment and Essential Supplies Inventory

Maintaining an up-to-date **Equipment Inventory and Essential Supplies Inventory** is a drill that gives you an edge before you travel to your competition event. Committing to this drill gives you the opportunity to train with your end goal in mind. Russell Wilson coined the phrase, "The Separation is in the Preparation." The time, effort, and strategy implementation that you invest into your preparation, before you compete, is an edge that will separate you from everyone else. I want to encourage you to start now, doing the things others are not willing to do.

You will never regret investing time committing to this drill. Should you be seeking an edge, this drill may be where you want to start. I have provided you with multiple open journaling pages to use to document and update your **Equipment and Essential Supplies Inventory.** The following is a breakdown of 4 transformational benefits which may help you gain your edge.

- Staying organized and keeping inventory stocked. Putting pen to paper is a great strategy to gain clarity and maintain quality control of what you have and what you will need. It is a disruption and a distraction to realize that you were not as prepared as you thought. This drill acts as your coach to remind you of the intricate details of your process so that you can trust your routine.
- Retain energy at an optimal level. Each time you make decisions you are taking a withdrawal from your energy account. As you pack your equipment and essential supplies, you may have asked yourself, "Do I need this?" or "Do I have enough of that?" Making decisions, no matter how big or small, each take withdrawals from your energy account. Having undeniable conviction knowing what you need and what you have, helps you to retain energy.
- Utilize time efficiently. Everyone gets the exact same amount of time: 168 hours each week and 86,400 seconds every day. Maintaining an inventory helps you pack for your event and keep track of your items, one time, instead of returning to your packing routine with multiple revisits, rechecks, and re-dos. Your time is valuable, and time is something you cannot replenish. This drill helps you streamline your process and become a savage of your time.
- Decrease anxiety and amplify focus. You compete at your optimal level when you are present. When you spend time

fretting about what you don't have and then worrying about how you are going to find what you need, these thoughts steal your focus away from your process of being present and competing. Maintaining an up-to-date inventory of your equipment and essential supplies helps you focus on what's important now – doing what you need to do to perform at your optimal level.

> *"The time is now; the place is here. You've got to be where you need to be, when you need to be there."*
> —DR. KEN RAVIZZA

Get to Know the Author...

Donene Taylor is a Wyoming cowgirl who remembers being fascinated by rodeo champions from the very start. All she ever talked about was, "The day she would get to go down the road and rodeo." At 14, she had a dream to become a World Champion, Tie-Down Calf Roper, in Women's Professional Rodeo. For the next 30+ years, she worked toward that dream. Along the way, she stalled, but she never stopped. At 52 years of age, Donene Taylor finally got what she had dreamed of. She became a World Champion, Tie-Down Calf Roper in the WPRA in 2016. She is also a 4-time WPRA Mountain States Circuit Champion Tie-down Calf Roper. She continues to live "happily ever after" with her husband, Stan, and sons, Hunter and Roper. As she puts it, they reside in one of the best small towns ever, Glenrock, Wyoming.

Today, Donene is a Certified Mental Performance Coach who transforms athletes from being goal setters to Bold Goal Getters! She teaches transformational mental performance strategies that help her athletes close the gap between where they are and where they want to be. She continues to compete with the most elite women rodeo athletes, in the world, in the Women's Professional Rodeo Association. Just like you, she has Bold Goals and is running them down, one step at a time.

Mental Performance Coach: Athletes of all ages and ability levels are utilizing Donene's one-on-one coaching program to help them achieve their bold goals, master their mental game, and WIN. Customized to take each athlete from where they are to where they want to be, Donene applies proven strategies to overcome their specific struggles.

Speaker: Donene Taylor's keynote speaking presentations are creative, innovative and engage the audience with fun, educational, and high energy, interactive exercises. Her energy, enthusiasm, and excitement are contagious. She will inspire and motivate the audience with impactful stories, and mental performance strategies that she shares from her heart. The audience will be empowered with mental performance strategies, which they will be able to implement immediately. Her goal is to help audience members mine for the gold that is already inside of them. Whether it's a large or small group, Donene is ready to help your group take the next step toward excellence.

Corporate Trainer: Empower your employees, at every level, with Donene Taylor's corporate training seminars. Either held in person or via Zoom, Donene delivers creative, personal, and actionable strategies to catapult your team to a higher and more elite level. Your employees will be given mental performance strategies, which they will be able to implement immediately. These strategies are delivered through interactive high-energy exercises and from personal storytelling. This unique combination engages the audience and gives them the tools they need to perform at their best.

Blog Writer: Enjoy Donene Taylor's blog series where she imparts wisdom, combined with humor, to teach lessons about running down your BOLD GOALS.

Author: In *Heart of a Champion*, Donene Taylor unpacks her journey, shares her mistakes, the lessons she learned, and how she grew, and evolved from each one. *Heart of a Champion* is her Mental Performance Playbook. With it, you'll learn how to live your life being all-in, going all out, and never holding back.

FOLLOW DONENE ON SOCIAL   @donenetaylor

SIGN UP FOR FREE RESOURCES AND NEWSLETTERS www.donenetaylor.com

INSPIRED
BY WHAT YOU READ?

Connect with Donene

FOLLOW DONENE ON SOCIAL

@donenetaylor

SIGN UP FOR FREE RESOURCES AND NEWSLETTERS

www.donenetaylor.com

CONTACT US AT

**donenetaylor@gmail.com
(307) 267-4824**

Mental Performance Coaching by Donene Taylor

ACHIEVE YOUR BOLD GOALS
CLOSE THE GAP

FROM WHERE YOU ARE

- Struggling to let go of mistakes/poor performance
- Unable to perform in competition like in practice
- Negative self-talk and thoughts
- Distracted and losing focus
- Paralyzed when competing with pressure

TO WHERE YOU WANT TO BE

- Master emotional regulation and resilience
- Compete with confidence and consistency
- Perform with positive self-talk and productive thoughts
- Perform with locked-in laser focus
- Compete at your best while having fun

Donene Taylor

- Certified Mental Performance Coach
- Author, *Heart of a Champion*
- WPRA World Champion

307-267-4824
donenetaylor@gmail.com

---

90 Day Coaching Program

6 1-on-1 Zoom Calls

DAILY Support Through Voxer & Email

"The book that will CHANGE YOUR LIFE"

—Lari Dee Guy
10X WORLD CHAMPION

GET YOUR COPY TODAY ON

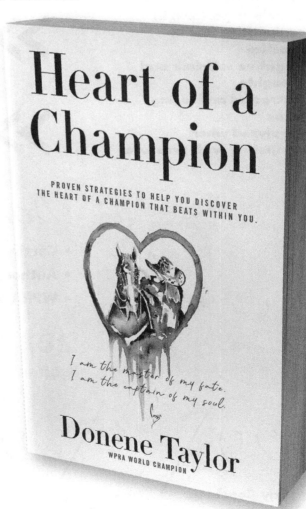

SCHEDULE A ONE-ON-ONE COACHING CALL

THE MENTAL PERFORMANCE PLAYBOOK

Heart of a Champion
READER REVIEWS

"It will change your life."
—LARI DEE GUY, 10X WORLD CHAMPION

"It will inspire you to get out and be productive."
—CONNLEE

"Do yourself a favor and just read it. If you're a competitor in any discipline, this book will encourage you beyond measure."
—NATALIE M.

*"A must read for mental performance. Parents, the best thing you can do for your competitive kids is train them to control their mind.
It will help them their whole life."*
—D.S.

"Life changing. I know it's a big statement, but this book is life changing. I'm not a roper and probably never will be but this book touched me on so many levels. Donene is an inspiration and proof that you can beat adversity and accomplish anything if you want it bad enough."
—AMAZON CUSTOMER

"Why I loved it so much?? It's real. Story of a struggle, highs and lows, quit and start... She is also a wife and a mom of two so I love how she kept her family involved in her world champion pursuit. It will make you think, it will make you tear up and it will offer strategies for digging deep and closing the gap between average and elite mindset. I highly recommend this book to all my athletes or anybody aspiring for greatness in any area of their life."
—NEVENA TAYLOR

"This book is incredibly inspiring! For every woman whatever the age, this book will capture you right away. Donene's story and her openness to share all she has learned along the way is priceless information for anyone. This book will help you discover your true journey in life, or at least light that spark inside of you!"
—JANELLE HANSON

"Heart of a Champion is a must read! Through Donene's life journey, God's grace and favor bring to life the ability to overcome obstacles, develop mindfulness, visualizing positive outcomes and tools that become instrumental in becoming the best version of ourselves that God has created each of us to be!!"
—ANGIE GREEN

Made in the USA
Las Vegas, NV
06 January 2024

84014455R00184